W9-ATC-913

DISCOVERING VIENNA THROUGH LEGENDS

HANNELORE TIK

TEXT & PRODUCTION: Hannelore Tik
EDITORIAL ASSISTANCE: Royston Nicholls
COMPUTER ASSISTANCE: Thomas Tik & Marcus Tik
COPYRIGHT: © 2000 Hannelore Tik
DESIGN: team concept
PRINTED IN AUSTRIA
• **PICTURES:**
• **Pablik Pictures,** A-1160 Vienna, Brunnengasse 33/11
  Tel. (+43/1)49 20 007 - front cover, back cover, as well as all
  other pictures except for those listed below.
• **Historisches Museum d. Stadt Wien,** A-1040 Vienna,
  Karlsplatz- http://www.museum.vienna.at -
  Tel. (+43/1) 505 87 47; pictures on page: 10, 11, 64, 67
• **Domkirche St. Stephan,** Kirchenmeisteramt , A-1010 Wien
• **Verlag Bauer,** A-1030 Vienna, Beatrixg.3
  Tel. (+43/1) 713 33 37; pictures on page: 23, 24, 28
• **Chorherrnstift Klosterneuburg,** Stiftsplatz 1,
  Tel. (+43) 2243/411 154
  http://www.stift.klosterneuburg.net;
  picture by Frau Kitlitschka page 145
• **Hannelore Tik,** page: 20, 85, 109, 112, 114, 115, 117, 138,
  139, 143

The book should be available at your local bookshop, but you
can also order it directly via fax (+43/1) 714 67 10 or
e-mail: hannelore-tik@netway.at

ISBN 3-9501263-0-9

To
My little Lisa
and all small children who live happily in the present
knowing little from the past.

ACKNOWLEDGEMENTS

I would like to express my gratitude to Canon Mons. Dr. Michael Willhelm, Church Office of St. Stephan for the permission to reproduce pictures and legends of the cathedral free of charge.

My gratitude also to Mag. Wolfgang Huber of the Klosterneuburg Stiftsmuseum for the permission to reproduce text and pictures of the Monastery free of charge.

My gratitude to H. Prof. Leander Petzold, University of Innsbruck, for the permission to reproduce text from his book: "Sagen aus Wien" free of charge.

I would also like to thank my sons Thomas, Marcus and Stefan for their unwavering support in all matters related to the book and their practical help in all the problems I encountered on the computer.

My dear friend Royston Nicholls, who patiently corrected my manuscript providing the text with the necessary touch of native English that makes it a pleasant read.

As well as my friend Wolfgang Pablik, who provided his expertise as a professional photographer to show you Vienna's sites perfectly.

All my friends who provided me with their good advice, support and belief in my project during its long preparation, especially for the financial support of the Dr. Günter Tik & Partner GmbH.

My special thanks and love to Wendy Hofmaier, MBE (co-founder of the British Bookshop and its Managing Director for twenty-five years), who kindly provided her expertise in all matters regarding the book.

More important however, I'd like to thank all the British Bookshop customers, who's repeated requests for a book on Vienna's legends actually triggered my wish to make it.

Last but not least, I'd like to express my gratitude to the management of the Prachner KG and The British Bookshop GmbH, Andreas Tarbuk and Pat Symonds, for their support.

INTRODUCTION

Walking through Vienna's First District - the City, as it's called nowadays - you'll frequently come across old stone figures, pillars, pictures and trade signs on house walls, as well as street names, that are reminders of times long gone by. You might ask yourself what they actually mean and why they have been left there for so many years, even centuries. Over the years, such questions have of course led to the blending of fact and fiction and in some cases legends have developed. Older Viennese might even be able to tell you some of these, but most of the younger people won't know them at all.

This book is a collection of the more well known and hopefully interesting legends that are still traceable in Vienna and its surroundings. Interesting as they are in themselves, I have described them in the form of individual walking tours around the related legendary sites, together with a brief history. For your convenience the recommended public transport starting points are also indicated. So why don't you accompany me on a discovery tour of Vienna's legends and history.

Vienna's history goes back to Roman times when it was called "Vindobona" and built as a Roman fort to protect this outpost of the Roman Empire against invading tribes from the East. During the reign of the House of Babenberg and later on of the Habsburgs,

Vienna developed from a well fortified city into a grand Baroque European capital with numerous beautiful palaces and churches most of which can still be explored today.
It was within the once thick city walls that many of the legends developed.

Bird's eye view of Vienna in 1683 by Hufnagel

(according to a copperplate engraving by Visher,
Historisches Museum der Stadt Wien, Karlsplatz)

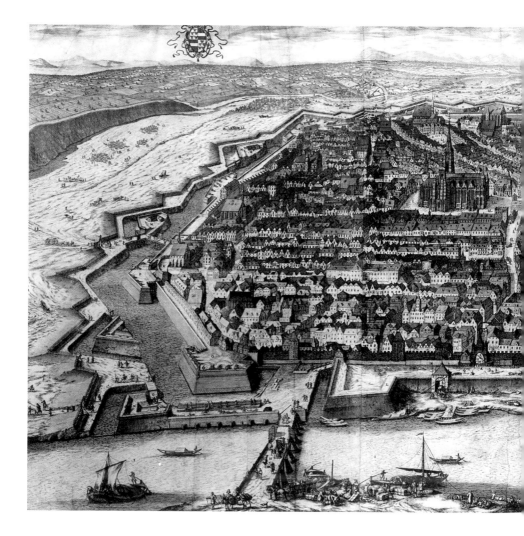

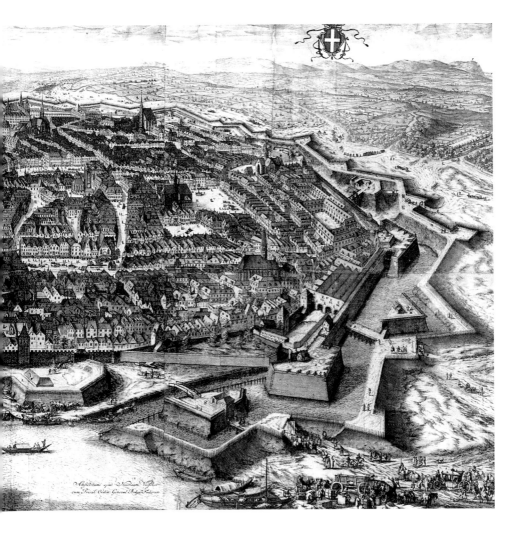

Aspestum apud Neustam Vipitenum
cum Praesid Civitae General Belgii Fodevum

11

ST. STEPHAN'S CATHEDRAL

STARTING POINT
U1, U3 Stephansplatz / City

Let's start our discovery tour at Vienna's landmark St. Stephan's Cathedral, which you just can't miss when you come into the city. Wherever you emerge from the Underground station you will immediately see the majestic cathedral with its high, arrow like spire in the middle of the big open square.

Many centuries ago the cathedral was just a little church surrounded by a few houses when, according to legend, the Babenberger Duke Heinrich Jasomirgott founded the cathedral after having a very special dream.

HEINRICH'S DREAM

One day while Duke Heinrich was hunting in the Leopoldsberg woods, just outside of Vienna, he came across an impressive deer in the distance and so he chased after it. The scared animal however, was quicker than he and eventually escaped into a thicket of woods. As Heinrich was exhausted after the hard chase, he settled down for a rest in a little clearing. From here he could enjoy the view of his father's castle on the Leopoldsberg on the one side and Vienna on the other side down in the Danube valley. Overcome by tiredness he soon fell asleep and began to dream.

In this dream he saw a handsome young man clad as a stone-mason. He had a compass and a set square tucked into his broad belt and was holding a piece of paper with a sketch of a beautiful cathedral in his hand. The young man told Heinrich that if he built a beautiful cathedral in place of the little church of Saint Stephan, it would bring him luck, and the cathedral would eventually stand in the middle of Vienna and become its proud landmark. However, just as Heinrich wanted to take the plan from him, he woke up and was left wondering what this dream could have meant.

Duke Heinrich could not forget the dream and finally decided to build a cathedral in place of the church and informed his Master stone-mason Oktavian of his plan. Oktavian accepted the Duke's order enthusiastically and work on the new cathedral was started immediately. After a few months however, Oktavian fell ill and was glad when a young stone-mason from Regensburg called Fridolin came to offer his help. Fridolin showed so much talent that master Oktavian soon entrusted him with the most difficult tasks and with his help the construction work proceeded quickly.

One day Duke Heinrich came into the Master mason's workshop to enquire about the progress of the cathedral and with great astonishment recognised Fridolin as the young man in his dream. On being asked who he was, Fridolin just told him that he was a simple stone-mason from Regensburg.

It took quite some years before the cathedral was completed, but finally it was ready for the inauguration.

A large crowd of people had gathered in Saint Stephan's Square to take part in the celebrations, but shortly before the inauguration Fridolin informed Master Oktavian that he must leave before the ceremony would start. He told him, that the work was completed and that there were many other cathedrals which required his help. Since this upset Master Oktavian very much he got Fridolin to promise that he would visit him at least once more before he dies.

Master Oktavian was able to enjoy the fruits of his great work for a few more years, before he felt his end coming near. On his death bed his only wish was to see Fridolin once more. Suddenly the door opened and the room was filled with a heavenly light, Fridolin had in fact come back and he approached Oktavian. Sensing the extreme light, the dying man opened his eyes once more and exclaimed: "Oh, Jesus, it was you who helped me to build Saint Stephan's" . Now filled with joy and satisfaction he sank back on his bed and died. So the legend goes.

In reality the construction of the cathedral actually took several centuries and was built 3 times in different styles. In the beginning it was a church built in early Romanesque style, founded by **Duke Heinrich II. "Jasomirgott"** and was consecrated to Saint Stephan in 1147. During the 12th century it was rebuilt in late

Romanesque style, but was badly damaged in the fire that ravaged Vienna in 1258. All that was left (which can still be seen today) is the **Riesentor (Giant's Doorway)** and its accompanying **Heiden Türme (Pagan Towers),** which were partly built with stones from the old Roman city walls. The reconstructed Romanesque cathedral was consecrated to Saint Stephan in 1263. Later on it was again rebuilt and enlarged in Gothic style according to the wishes of the then reigning monarch, **Duke Rudolph IV,** the Founder (1339 -1365). He wanted a majestic cathedral with two very high spires. This time the reconstruction took almost 150 years until the 137 meter high South Tower was finished under the guidance of Master stone-mason Hans Prachatitz in 1433. At the same time his stone-mason Hans Puchsbaum built the complicated vaulted roof of the nave and also started the construction of the North Tower. The North Tower however, was never finished and was capped with a Renaissance roof in 1578 when all hope had been abandoned to complete it in the same style as the South Tower.

The unfinished North Tower

Go to the left of the cathedral, where the horse carriages line up for customers and see for yourself how much lower the **North Tower** is compared to the tower on the other side. Even from here you can see the **South Tower** rising far over the cathedral roof. Why wasn't the **North Tower** built like the **South Tower?** The real answer is probably that the city and the emperor ran out of money, but legend about Master Puchsbaum's fate would have us believe differently.

HANS PUCHSBAUM'S FATE

Hans Puchsbaum was a stone-mason at St. Stephan's cathedral, making pillars and altars with finely carved figures and decorations on them. Master Prachatitz, the Master stonemason, was very satisfied with his work and even entrusted him with the construction of the huge nave. However, Hans was not only working hard, he was also in love with the Master's daughter Mary and wanted to marry her. Mary loved him too and so he asked the Master, if he would allow them to become man and wife.

Master Prachatitz, who's wife had recently died, loved his only daughter very much and did not want to give her away so easily. He therefore challenged Hans with an enormous task, such that he would only be allowed to marry Mary, if he managed to build the North Tower as big as the South Tower within one year.

At first poor Hans was shocked by this demand, but since he loved her so much, agreed to take on the challenge and prove himself worthy of the master's daughter and started the new task immediately.

At first the building of the new tower developed quite well, but Hans soon realised that they were not fast enough to finish it within a year. He grew more and more anxious and checked the building work himself every night. Once, while he was working desperately to complete the work on the tower, an ugly old man in a black coat and a red hat joined him. After watching him for a while and asking him all sorts of questions, the old man offered to finish the tower for him within the requested time. Although Hans didn't really believe that the man could do this, he asked him what he would want in exchange for it. The old man just asked him to promise never again to mention the name of God or any other holy names in his life, otherwise the old man would take his soul. Hans thought that this couldn't be so difficult and accepted the offer. From that time on, the construction work progressed much more quickly.

The Viennese, walking past the cathedral almost every day, suddenly noticed that the work was being completed extremely fast and whispered that only the Devil could work at such speed. Was the old man in fact the Devil?

Hans Puchsbaum and the Devil

Der Turmbau von St. Stephan.

During the months of intensive work on the tower, Hans had not been able to see his beloved Mary.

All the greater was his joy, when one day he suddenly noticed her crossing the square. He leaned over the scaffolding and tried to attract her attention by shouting her name: "Mary, Mary!" Unfortunately, this was not only her name, but also the name of the "Virgin Mary", a holy name which he had promised not to use. Immediately the plank under his feet gave way and Hans plunged to the ground, the whole scaffolding collapsing on top of him, fulfilling the devil's curse.

The terrible event shocked the people of Vienna so much that the North Tower was never finished to the height of the South Tower.

The Giant's Doorway

Before you enter the church at **the Riesentor (Giant's Doorway),** take a closer look at it. You will discover for instance, some square niches with strange looking figures in them. We do not know the meaning of all of them, but the one looking as if he is removing a thorn from his foot is known as **Dornauszieher (Thorn-remover)** and is said to depict a judge.

In the Middle Ages churches were not only places of worship, but also places of judgement. This is emphasised by the figure above the door, which depicts Jesus as the judge of the world, seated in a ray of glory, holding the book of life in his left hand, while his right hand is raised in blessing. Two angels and the apostles look up to him as their judge and ruler.

The **circular shape** worn into the wall to the left of the door presents another riddle to solve. It might just have been the result of a large door hinge rubbing on the wall, but it could also have been made purposely to be used as an official measurement for the size of bread at that time. Did the people really come here to see if the bread they had bought was actually the right size? Read the story of the punishment for bakers who sold under-sized bread later in the book. Just underneath this circle we see two iron bars of different lengths which might have also been used as measurement standards, perhaps by the stone-masons and the architects of the cathedral. Who knows?

Once inside the cathedral you see immediately its full size, as the three different naves are only separated by massive pillars instead of walls, which makes it look like one huge room. The church hall is 34 meters wide and at its highest point 28 m high.

The **cathedral** is richly decorated with many statues, grave stones and altars; of which I would like to point out only a few. Just inside the entrance on the second pillar to the left we see the Gothic pulpit built by the **Master stone-mason Anton Pilgram** in the years 1510 to 1515. If you take a closer look at the pulpit you will find a self-portrait of the Master underneath the staircase, where he carved himself looking out of a window frame. This is called the "Fenstergucker".

Master Pilgram at the Pulpit

Pilgram decorated the balustrade of the pulpit with little creatures fighting each other on their way up towards the watchdog at the highest point. These figures are meant to remind the priests of all the evil things happening in the world. From the pulpit's balustrade the so **called "Four Fathers of the Church" (St. Ambrose, St. Jerome, St. Gregory and St. Augustine)** watch us from their special high vantage place.

Master Pilgram at the original organ.

On the wall to the left of the pulpit, where the original organ was situated, we see another self-portrait of **Master Pilgram.** Here he looks across the church holding his instruments, a compass and a set square.

Unfortunately the original organ was damaged and had to be removed. Today's organ with its 10,000 pipes is situated above the main entrance and is said to be one of the most modern and largest in the world.

Old picture of the "Toothache Lord"

Just around the corner from Master Pilgram's self-portrait we find the statue of the **suffering Lord,** which is placed high above our heads in a dark corner by the entrance to the North Tower. In German this statue is called **Zahnweh Herrgott (Toothache Lord)** and was originally placed on an outside wall of the church, where poor people used to kneel down for a short prayer before hurrying on with their business. The following legend tells us how the statue got its name.

THE TOOTHACHE LORD

L ong ago, when the statue of the **suffering Lord** was still placed outside the cathedral, a young woman came regularly to pray to Jesus there. One day she decorated his head with a wreath of flowers which she fixed around his head with some ribbons, so that they wouldn't be blown away by the wind. In the evening three drunken young men passed the statue on their way home from a party. The first who saw the flower wreath joked mockingly: " Look, the Lord has a toothache.", the other one said: "No surprise, he stands in a draught all day long" and the third said: "He will have to have his tooth pulled out." Laughingly they went and didn't think of it anymore. Later at home, Leopold, one of these men, wanted to go to sleep immediately. However he couldn't fall asleep and tossed and turned in his bed for some time before he suddenly developed a terrible toothache. He got up angrily and took a large gulp of spirits to kill the pain, but the pain didn't stop and in the end he had to call a doctor. The doctor however, who could not find the reason for his pain, said: "You are the third man complaining to me about such a toothache. You must have all caught the tooth plague and this is an illness I cannot treat. Only the Lord Almighty can help you, which he might do if you ask him nicely." Leopold remembered his mocking remarks the evening before and knew now that his toothache was his punishment for it. Full of remorse he went to the Lord's statue, where he surprisingly also found his two friends. They kneeled down together and asked the Lord for forgiveness for their mockery.

People passing by laughed about the three naughty friends kneeling in the street before the Lord's statue. The Lord however, forgave them and cured their pain.

You can only get a closer look of the impressively gilded side altar called **the Wiener Neustädter Altar (Altar of Wiener Neustadt)** situated at the end of the Women's Nave, by taking a guided tour. The altar was donated by Emperor Friedrich III in 1447, but stayed in Wiener Neustadt until 1884 when it was finally moved to the cathedral in Vienna.

The **High Altar** shows the patron of the church, Saint Stephan, being stoned to death outside Jerusalem. Heaven above him is already wide open for his ascension; Jesus, seated to the right of the Father, awaits him. The altar was made of black marble by the brothers **Tobias** and **Johann Jakob Pock** between 1640 and 1660. The altar was consecrated in 1647, and since that time the patron saint's day is celebrated on December 26th. The statues beside the **High Altar** (see below) are the patron saints of Vienna, namely St. Leopold, St. Florian, St. Roch and St. Sebastian.

Walking a little further in the direction towards the South Tower, our attention is drawn to a grave stone with the statue of **Emperor Friedrich III. (1440 - 1493).** During his reign, Vienna was captured by the Hungarian king Calvin and the emperor fled to Wiener Neustadt, where he stayed until the Hungarian king's death in 1490 before returning to Vienna. The grave stone itself is decorated with his coat of arms and his famous initials A.E.I.O.U., which are said to stand for his personal motto. There are several interpretations for these famous initials, such as: "Austriae Est Imperare Orbi Universo" (It is for Austria to rule the entire world) or "Austria Erit In Orbe Ultima" (Austria will outlast all other powers). Both of these would have perfectly described Austria's importance during his reign.

Servant's Madonna with child.

Even if you do not take a guided tour to the special altars, you can still see the famous 14th century statue of the Madonna with Child (near the exit to the South Tower) which is called „**Dienstboten Muttergottes**".

As this lovely old statue is said by legend to have helped a poor servant in a desperate situation, it is still the most frequently visited place in the cathedral.

THE SERVANT'S MADONNA

Once upon a time a rich, but very vain lady lived in Vienna. She had a beautiful Madonna statue in her house and used to pray to it very often. Despite this she was not a really good Christian because she was very nasty and unforgiving to her servants, especially to a young orphan girl, who had to endure all her moodiness.

One day the lady wanted to go out dressed in her best clothes and wearing her most valuable necklace. The young girl was told to bring her all of these things, but she could not find the necklace as it was not in the jewellery box. The lady accused the girl of having stolen her necklace and sent for the police to arrest her. The poor girl, who had actually done nothing wrong, could not prove her innocence and so she prayed to the Madonna for help. The lady saw her and remarked scornfully that the Madonna was not responsible for mere servants and would not listen to her prayers. The police however, did not immediately arrest the girl, but started to search all the rooms of the house. They finally found the precious necklace hidden in a suitcase that belonged to a groom. The terribly embarrassed lady promised to treat the girl better in future and as an act of gratitude donated her Madonna statue to the Cathedral, where it was given a special place.

Before leaving the church you can take a guided tour down into the **Catacombs,** which are basically the imperial vaults of the House of Habsburg. However, you will also see the skulls and bones of thousands of Viennese piled up there. During the time of wars, when too many people died in a short period of time, the cemetery around the church was often not big enough to bury them all. Old graves had to be opened to make room for the new corpses and the old bones were piled up in the catacombs for their final rest.

The main attraction however, is the **Imperial Ducal Vault,** where the members of the House of Habsburg were buried. **Rudolph IV. the Founder (1339 -1365)** reigned for only 7 years, but was one of the most powerful and important emperors of the Habsburg dynasty. The completion of the reconstruction of the Romanesque basilica into a Gothic cathedral was his main ambition in life. He not only laid the cornerstone for the Gothic expansion of the cathedral, but is even said to have dug the first spade of sod for the new tower in 1359. He also decided to have the Imperial

Vault built in the cathedral. A legend tells us how he informed his brothers of this intention.

RUDOLPH'S IMPERIAL DUCAL VAULT

One day Emperor Rudolph asked his two brothers, Leopold and Albrecht, to meet him at the cathedral. He led them to a place in front of the High Altar where they were taken down into a deep vault which he had constructed. Here Rudolph said to them: "My beloved brothers! I am reconstructing this great cathedral in honour to the Lord Almighty. The Cathedral shall be a sign of our belief in God for centuries to come. I brought you here to show you this vault, which is intended to be the burial place of all Emperors of the House of Habsburg in future. Give me your solemn promise to bury me here, as the first of the Habsburg Emperors and also assure me that you will finish the cathedral according to my plans" and they both promised to do so. Some time later Rudolph died on his way back from Italy after marrying his second wife. His bereaved brothers brought him back to Vienna and buried him as the first Emperor in the vault of St. Stephan's Cathedral, thus fulfilling one of their promises.

Since the House of Habsburg ruled for so long (from 1276 to 1918) the vault was not big enough for all the Habsburg Emperors. It therefore became custom to keep only copper urns with their intestines in St. Stephan's Cathedral. Their actual bodies were buried in the **Imperial Vault** at the **Kapuzinerkirche (Capuchin Church),** while their hearts were buried in silver urns in **the Heart Vault** at the **Ausgustinerkirche (Church of the Augustinians).** This means that the bodies of most Habsburg Emperors are not buried like other people in one piece, but at three different burial sites.

Coming back up from the **Catacombs** you can take the lift up to the top of the **North Tower** to see the cathedral's largest bell, the **"Pummerin".** This big bell, weighing about 20 tons, is only rung at very special events such as every New Year's Eve. The original Pummerin was cast from the metal of the cannons that were left after the Turkish siege of Vienna in 1683. What you see today is actually the second cast of the bell, as the original was destroyed together with large parts of the cathedral in the last days of the Second World War in 1945.

For the bell's reconstruction the pieces of the old shattered bell were used as well. From the top of Master Puchsbaum's unfinished North Tower you can enjoy the view of today's Vienna.

The much higher and more impressive **South Tower** by

Master Hans Prachatiz has no lift, but can be climbed via its 343 stairs. The rather strenuous climb is however well worth it, as it gives you an even better view of the city surrounding the cathedral. The view stretches from the Vienna Woods in the west including its last mountain, Leopoldsberg, at the edge of the Danube, as well as far beyond the Danube plains to the east, and to the south as far as to the Schneeberg mountain lying some 80 km from Vienna.

St. Stephan's weathercock

Much nearer, at the end of the cathedral's roof, you can see a weathercock turning in the wind, which leads us to the legend of a brave knight.

THE WEATHERCOCK OF ST. STEPHAN'S

In the 15th century a brave knight named Kaspar lived with his wife at the Duke's court in Vienna. They loved each other dearly and never wanted to be parted. However one day the knight was ordered to travel together with other knights to Turkey to bring the Sultan a message from the Austrian Duke. The knight was very unhappy that he had to go on such a long and dangerous journey, but it couldn't be helped, since it was an order. Before parting from his wife, he begged her to wait for him faithfully and not to be distracted by other young knights who might use foul tricks to make her believe that he had died so that they could marry her. She promised that she would only remarry after receiving the silver cross, which he always wore around his neck, as a clear sign that he had actually died.

While in the Turkish capital, the knight was unfortunately abducted and sold as a slave. His comrades, who returned safely to Vienna, were afraid of being punished for not preventing his abduction; so they told everybody that he had died and been buried in Turkey.

His wife mourned him for three years refusing to accept any approaches by other knights. Deep down she still hoped that her dear husband would return home one day, since she had not received his silver cross from his comrades.

During all those years while the knight was kept as a slave in Turkey his dear wife was always in his thoughts. One night he dreamed of attending the wedding of his wife to one of his comrades in St. Stephan's cathedral the very next day. Awakening from

34

his dream he moaned: "I would give away my soul if only I could be in Vienna tomorrow." As soon as he had spoken those careless words, a cock crowed and the Devil appeared in front of his bed. "Get up, get up!", he shouted "if you promise to be mine in body and soul, I'll take you on that cock to Vienna and you'll be there before the sun rises tomorrow!"

The knight, who believed that the silver cross would still protect him, thought it over for a second and replied: "Well, I agree but under the condition that I am still asleep upon arrival in Vienna, otherwise you shall not have me." The Devil agreed to do it under this condition and after a short prayer the knight fell deeply asleep again. The Devil immediately told the cock to fly the knight at high speed to Vienna, before he could wake up again.

Next day the Devil was already waiting for his victim, but unfortunately for the Devil the cock started to crow loudly at sun rise which awakened the knight just before he arrived in Vienna. Oh, what joy, he had woken up before arriving in Vienna and therefore escaped the Devil. He soon saw the tower of St. Stephan's where the cock landed shortly afterwards. The Devil was very angry that he had lost his victim, and couldn't hold on to his soul. The knight went straight home where he happily found his wife faithfully waiting for him and not planning to get married as in his dream.

Thankful for his deliverance, he asked a blacksmith to make a cock like the one he had returned on and had it placed on the roof of St. Stephan's.

When you return from the **"Steffl"**, as the Viennese have nicknamed the **South Tower**, you should make a little detour into **Churhausgasse** opposite, from where one has a perfect view of the church's roof. It shows **the Imperial Double Eagle** of the former monarchy of Austria - Hungary with the Emperor's initials "F. I." in the middle, and "1831" the date of its reconstruction. If you then walk through Singerstraße and then a little way into the Graben, you'll get a complete view of the majestic cathedral roof. It was restored using approximately 230.000 new glazed tiles after the damage of the Second World War.

LEGENDS ON FOOT

STARTING POINT
U1, U3 Stephansplatz / City

We can continue our exploration of the oldest parts of the city right here on Stephansplatz. This time we would like to find more hidden places and signs of the city's past when it was still a small town protected by strong city walls and a moat. To orientate yourselves in all those narrow lanes, take a close look at a map before you start and see if you can locate all the street names I have listed below as a path finder for my recommended route:

Stephansplatz, Stock im Eisen - Platz,
Graben, Pest Säule (Plague Column)
Bognergasse, past the square Am Hof
corner Heidenschuß / Strauchgasse
Tiefer Graben - "Hohe Brücke"-
Maria Am Gestade (church) on Passauer Platz
Stoß Im Himmel Gasse
Wipplinger Straße (Old Town Hall)
Hoher Markt (Anker Clock)
Judengasse to Ruprechtskirche (church)
a detour to Stern Gasse and back to Ruprechtskirche
stairs down to Schwedenplatz, or walk down
Seitenstettengasse to Schwedenplatz

Rotenturm Straße, first left into Griechengasse
Griechengasse / Fleischmarkt (Inn "Lieber Augustin")
Schönlaterngasse (house with "Basilisk")
Heiligenkreuzer Hof (the monastery's courtyard is
open to the public), via Fleischmarkt to
Rotenturm Straße (picture of the "Red Tower")
via **Stephansplatz** to
Singerstraße , first left Blutgasse to
Domgasse, via Grünangergasse back to Singerstraße
Seilerstätte, past the "British Bookshop" in
Weihburggasse, up to Himmelpfortgasse to
Winter Palace of Prince Eugene.
Himmelpfortgasse down to the Ring and the
Schwarzenbergplatz; tram line D goes to the
Belvedere Palace in Prinz Eugen Straße.

Stock-im-Eisen-Platz (Iron-Stump-Square) is the
part of Stephansplatz which joins Kärntner Straße
and Graben. It derives its strange name from the
remaining stump of an old oak tree into which nails
were hammered centuries ago. We can still see this
relic of Mediaeval times on the corner of the house
Kärntner Straße / Graben (now protected by a glass
case). This stump of oak is seen to be a trade sign
of the Vienna guild of locksmiths. Every locksmith's
journeyman would hammer a nail into this oak tree,
that stood near the mediaeval city wall, before leaving
the city to take up his trade somewhere else. Even today

workmen are aware of that custom, and so it happened that by special permission the last nail was hammered into the stump by the builders of the Underground station Stephansplatz, when they had finished and went on to work somewhere else.

The original stump of an oak tree

Before telling you the legend of that custom, I'd like to explain some of the background about the old apprenticeship system here. Practically everything we use nowadays is mass produced by machines using practically no skilled hand-workers. This was not so in Medieval times when everything was made by hand in small workshops with very simple tools. A young man who wanted to become a locksmith, stone-mason, carpenter, goldsmith, baker or anything else had to serve as an apprentice to learn that trade from a Master for several years.

At the end of his apprenticeship the boy had to produce

his "master piece", as a proof of his acquired skills. If the Master was satisfied with it, the apprentice was declared a free journeyman who was supposed to travel away and work in the trade abroad. After some years travelling and gaining experience, he was allowed to return home where he could open his own workshop and be declared a Master himself.

THE IRON STUMP

One day a young locksmith's apprentice named Martin was sent to fetch some loam from a pit outside the city walls. Unfortunately he played around with other boys instead of completing his task quickly and so he was too late to reach the city gates before they were closed at sunset. Standing outside the gates, without any money to pay the guards to reopen them, he cried bitterly. Suddenly a little man in a red coat enquired what the problem was and offered him the money to get back into the city. He also offered to help him become a skilful locksmith if he promised to go to Holy Mass every Sunday for the rest of his life. Martin, who was glad of this offer to be able to return home before dark, gave the promise without a second thought.

Next day the stranger appeared at his Master's workshop and asked for a special lock that would be impossible to be opened without the proper key. The Master refused to accept this job as it seemed impossible to him. However, Martin who felt obliged to the stranger and remembered the man's offer to help him, suggested that his master allow him to attempt this task. His Master was at first angry, but finally agreed that the young apprentice should try anyway and find out for himself that not everything is possible and gave him the necessary material. After several hours of hard work on the anvil Martin surprisingly succeeded in making such a lock and key. When the stranger collected the lock, he got Martin to fix an old oak tree with this lock permanently against the city wall on the Graben. Martin wanted to keep the key, but the man took it and disappeared. His Master, who was amazed and shocked by his success, immediately declared him a free journeyman despite the fact that he hadn't served all his apprentice years. Due to this incredible event it now occurred to Martin that he had probably made a pact with the Devil.

So Martin started to travel from city to city where he was always welcomed at first, but people soon became afraid of his astonishing skills and sent him away again. After some years of travelling he decided to return to his home town Vienna, where he heard that the town council members were actually very annoyed that they could not remove the oak tree because no one could open this lock. Martin offered to make them a key, but the Devil who didn't want this to happen, continually interfered with his work such that each key was always the wrong way round. Eventually Martin managed to trick the Devil, so that the key came out of the fire the right way round. Martin triumphed and then showed the town council that this new key worked in the lock. Full of joy about his success he threw the key high up into the air, but surprisingly it never came back down to earth! The Devil had taken the key again. For some time Martin lived happily with his family as a successful locksmith, only regretting his pact with the Devil in as far as having to attend Mass every Sunday, which he carefully did. This annoyed the Devil since it seemed that he would not get Martin's soul after all. In a last attempt he encouraged Martin to take up drinking and gambling. One Sunday morning Martin's friends persuaded him to stay a little bit longer to finish a card game. Suddenly Martin remembered his duty to attend Mass and ran to church thinking he would be late.

Meeting an old woman standing outside the church he asked if the mass was still being celebrated, which it was, but she lied telling him that it had not yet started. Wishing to finish his game Martin returned to the inn, thinking that there would still be a Mass before Noon. However, suddenly he heard the bells of the church chime noon and then realised that he had been cheated and had missed the last chance of the day. This was the end of Martin, who was grabbed by the Devil and flown away. In the evening his smashed and torn body was found near the old oak tree.

Since that time it became a custom that every new locksmith's journeyman, would hit a nail into the old oak tree in order to remind them of poor Martin's fate.

Walking up the busy pedestrian area, the **Graben (the Moat),** we are actually walking along the path of the moat that ran around the Roman fortification walls of Vindobona, which was much smaller than Medieval Vienna.

The column that stands right in the middle of the Graben and is decorated with angels, clouds and the golden rays of sun on its top, is called **Pest Säule (Plague Column).** It is a symbol of the emperor's gratitude for the end of the plague that killed many thousands of Viennese in the 17th century. People died of it in such large numbers that they had to be buried in huge mass graves outside the city walls, as the usual cemeteries around the churches were far too small. Unfortunately the plague returned once more to Vienna, again killing many thousands of people before it disappeared completely. This time the emperor vowed to have a church erected as soon as it was over and the grand Baroque church **Karlskirche** was then built on Karlsplatz (see picture on page 153).

The Plague Column in the Graben

At the end of the **Graben** turn into **Bognergasse (Archery Maker's Lane),** which leads to the largest square of the inner city called **Am Hof (At Court).**

Today the square **Am Hof** is dominated by the Baroque church **Nine Choirs of Angels** and the Vienna **fire brigade's headquarters** (situated here since the 16th century). In early times the square had a much greater importance than today.

The Romans set up camp on this site and later the Babenbergers moved their court from the castle on the Leopoldsberg to this square in Vienna (1135-50). A plaque on the house Am Hof 2 tells us of the days of knights and ballad singers. You can read more about the Babenberger dynasty in the chapter "Kings and Queens of Austria".

Leave **Am Hof** by walking down the lane to the corner **Heidenschuß (Pagan's Shot)/ Strauchgasse,** where we can see the stone figure of a Turkish soldier on horseback swinging his dangerously curved sword.

This stone figure is one of the many reminders of that difficult period when Vienna was besieged by the Turkish army in 1529 and again in 1683. On both occasions the Viennese were able to hold out until the Turks eventually left. After the first siege in 1529 the old fortified walls were rebuilt and re-enforced to protect the city better against future threats from the east.

Pagan's shot at Heidenschuß

In 1683 the Turkish army under their leader Sultan Cara Mustapha returned to try again to conquer Vienna and place the Half Moon instead of the Christian cross on Saint Stephan's Cathedral. After many weeks of siege, the Viennese were finally freed by the Christian relief armies under the Polish King Jan Sobieski. It was during the first Turkish siege of Vienna that the house **Heidenschuss / Strauchgasse** became a legend.

PAGAN'S SHOT

In 1529 the Turkish Sultan Sueleyman attempted to conquer Vienna by surrounding the city with thousands of soldiers who attacked the city walls ferociously from all sides for many weeks.

The Viennese suffered terribly, since they did not have enough food for such a long siege. There weren't enough men to defend the city either, so people could only pray and hope for help from outside. To make things worse, a rumour went round that the Turks were digging tunnels to undermine the city walls and blow them up. Therefore, people who had their houses near the city walls, were told to watch out for unusual noises or vibrations in their cellars. Many put barrels covered with calf-skin down into the cellars and laid small dices onto them. If the dice should start to dance on the calf-skin, then it could be a sign that the Turks were digging near by.

One night, a baker was in his cellar baking bread for the hungry people, when he suddenly noticed that the dice on his barrel were moving slightly. The baker kneeled down, listened carefully and was soon convinced that he heard strange voices talking underneath the cellar floor. So he ran quickly to the nearest military post and reported it. Although the guards found it difficult to believe that the Turks were already so close, soldiers were immediately sent to the bakery where they flooded the cellar with water and waited nearby. When the Turks finally managed to break through the cellar floor they had no chance to escape the water and soon the soldiers heard the terrible cries of the drowning Turkish soldiers. When it was quiet again the soldiers searched the cellar for survivors, but found only dead bodies. Later the tunnel was filled in and closed so that the Turks could not use it again.

Soon after that event the Turkish Sultan decided to end the siege and left Vienna for Istanbul, where he had to pay with his life for not succeeding.

So it happened that an attentive baker saved Vienna from dreadful slaughter by the Turkish army.

Back to present times, we are now walking along the street called **Tiefer Graben (Deep Moat)** continuing the path of the moat that surrounded the Roman city walls. Where the street is spanned by an overhead bridge **"Hohe Brücke"**, we could climb up to the bridge via some public stairs to **Wipplinger Straße** which would lead us to the street called **Hoher Markt,** the oldest square in Vienna.

However, if you follow the old Roman moat **Tiefer Graben** you see on the right hand side a small Gothic church **"Maria Am Gestade" (Mary at the Strand)** situated several meters higher than the Tiefer Graben.

The fishermen's church „Maria am Gestade"

In former times fishermen, boatmen and other traders, who came down the Danube brought their goods into the city via the stairs called the **Fischer-stiege (Fisher-men's stairs)** and thanked the Holy Mary there for their safe journey.

We now go round the church to the right hand side and turn into the second lane left called **Stoß-im-Himmel-Gasse,** which reminds us of a legend about vanity, greed and arrogance:

PUSHED TO HEAVEN

Many years ago a very vain, greedy and arrogant woman lived in Vienna. Having nothing but her beauty on her mind, she would sit all day in front of her mirror admiring herself in her wonderful clothes. Instead of caring for her

49

household and family, her only interest was to be more beautiful than all the other women and to be admired by everybody.

One day she walked past a picture of the Virgin Mary and in her endless arrogance she sneered at the Virgin saying: "You in your modest dress can't compete with me because I am so beautiful, especially in this wonderful dress!" For a moment the woman thought that Mary actually looked away angrily, but then she concluded that it had only been an illusion and walked on with a proud smile on her face. But the wicked woman was soon to be punished for her mockery. It happened that an old poorly dressed beggar woman knocked at the vain woman's door at midnight. At first she scolded her for disturbing her in the middle of the night, but then the beggar woman showed her an amazingly beautiful dress and of course she wanted it immediately. However, she knew that she couldn't afford it as she had already spent her allowance that month, but surprisingly the beggar woman didn't want any money for it. She offered to let her have the dress for three days and three nights, after which she would have to return it to the beggar woman with whatever was still in the dress. The greedy woman agreed without thinking what that could possibly mean.

During the next three days she enjoyed showing off her new dress to all her friends. However, during the third night she started to think more about the promise she had given and it occurred to her that there might actually be a curse on the dress. So she immediately tried to get out of it, but it stuck to her body as if glued. She then tried desperately to tear off the dress, but unsuccessfully and was in great distress when the door was opened at midnight by the beggar woman coming to claim her dress back. The beggar woman laughed scornfully at her: "You promised to give me the dress and what is in it at midnight, and now you are in it yourself and you are mine!" The beautiful dress then spontaneously caught fire and the woman fought even more desperately to get it off pulling it apart at the neck. In doing so she exposed a cross and a picture of the Virgin Mary that she wore around her neck, which broke the curse. She then felt a strong push away from the beggar woman and the dress burst open and fell off her body thus saving her life. Following this she truly regretted her extreme vanity and did penance for her sins by becoming a nun in a monastery. In the end even the little religious belief that she had, had saved her life and pushed her towards heaven.

Leaving the site of the vain woman, we now turn towards the house at the corner of **Wipplinger Straße.** In the courtyard of the **Alte Rathaus (Old Town Hall)** we can have a look at the perhaps oldest house sign in Vienna, a Gothic stone angel holding the Vienna coat of arms with its white cross on a red background. In his other hand the angel holds the old Austrian coat of arms which shows the imperial eagle (see below).

The old town hall, which is still used for municipal purposes for the first district, has been replaced by the much larger "Rathaus" building on the Ring.

At the end of **Wipplinger Straße** we reach the centre of the old Roman city, called **Hoher Markt (High Market).** The street to the left at the traffic lights is called **Marc-Aurel-Straße** in commemoration of the Roman Emperor Marcus Aurelius, who died in Vienna while it was an outpost of the Roman empire. Remains of old Roman houses that once stood on this site are still to be seen in the museum situated underneath today's square, the entrance to which is at house No. 3.

You can also see a sculpture of this Roman emperor seated in his lion-drawn carriage next to the Secession in Friedrichstraße, near Karlsplatz. The square Hoher Markt was a main trading centre, where fishermen sold their freshly caught fish. For some time it was also favoured by the textile dealers of the nearby Jewish quarter; but more importantly it was also used as a place of judgement where executions were carried out in public. The little lane called **Rot Gasse (Red Lane),** at the right hand end of the **Hohe Markt,** is spanned by an archway decorated with a special clock, the **Anker Uhr (Anchor Clock),** so called after the Anker Insurance Company next to it (see below).

The clock high above the street is particularly attractive because of the individual historical figures that turn out at every hour. At noon they all perform a procession together with chimes. These figures depict such people as the Roman Emperor Marcus Aurelius; Master Hans Puchsbaum (an architect of St. Stephan's Cathedral); Count Starhemberg and Prince Eugene (both of whom defended Vienna during the Turkish siege); Empress Maria Theresia and Emperor Francis I. A plaque on the wall of the building lists the figures in their chrono-logical order and indicate when they will appear on the clock. After that romantic look at history we should go back to the middle of the square. Just behind the fountain is **Judengasse (Jew's Lane)** which is part of Vienna's Jewish quarter and houses Vienna's main Synagogue.

An extension to Judengasse forms Ruprechtsplatz and on the right just before the stairs down to the Danube Canal, stands Vienna's oldest church, called **Ruprechts Kirche (St. Ruprecht's Church).**
The small, old church overgrown with ivy dates back to the 11th century when it was dedicated to the bishop Saint Ruprecht of whom we can see a little statue next to the church entrance.

St. Ruprecht's Church

This was also a natural boundary of the Roman city, where it was protected by a sidearm of the Danube. Standing on this part of the old city walls it is easy to imagine looking over the moat (not today's busy Schwedenplatz) towards the Danube, where ships were unloaded and goods brought up to the market square. Since we are here near the Danube Canal, I'd also like to tell you the story of the punishment for bakers who sold undersized bread.

A BAKER'S PUNISHMENT

In the middle ages the standard loaf of bread was round shaped. If people thought that it was not as big as it should be, they went to St. Stephan's Cathedral and held their bread against the round shape next to the Giant's Doorway. If it turned out to be smaller than the circle on the church wall, they could go to the baker's guild with their complaint. If the complaint was justified, the baker was punished very severely and cruelly. He would be locked in a wooden cage fixed onto a long pole, which extended from the riverbank far into the river. The poor man would then be lowered into the water several times and each time left under water for some significant time. Although it was not meant to kill them, many bakers drowned.

Back to our walk you can either take the stairs near the church or go around Ruprechtskirche and take a closer look at all the popular inns in Seitenstettengasse which leads to Schwedenplatz.

Continue past the houses on **Schwedenplatz** until reaching the corner of **Rotenturm Straße** and walk up to the first street on the left, which is actually only a little lane called **Griechengasse.**

A Mediaeval lane: Griechengasse

This old narrow lane has some houses dating from the 13th century and one of them boasts a coat of arms of the year 1476.

Since this lane was always so narrow, the old house walls had to be protected from damage by horse drawn carriages with slabs of stones (today the lane is closed to traffic and only pedestrians can walk through). The house at the very corner with **Fleischmarkt (Meat Market)** was once a very popular inn, called the Red Roof Inn, where many musicians liked to stay. Nowadays it is called **Griechenbeisl (Greeks' Inn).**

A life size statue of the Viennese's most beloved ballad singer and bag piper "Der Liebe Augustin" is fixed to the house wall of the Inn and reminds us of the legend of this lucky man who survived a night in a mass grave during the time of the plague.

Bagpipe-player „Lieber Augustin"

DEAR AUGUSTIN

Augustin was a happy ballad singer who toured Vienna's inns entertaining people with jokes, songs and funny stories. He played his bag pipes to help people forget their fear of that strange illness that killed so many of them every day.

Because of his humour and happiness the Viennese loved him dearly, they called him **Lieber Augustin (Dear Ausgustin),** but even he became sad when fewer and fewer people came to the inns to listen to him. One night he drowned his sorrow in wine and in his drunken state he was unable to walk home properly, so that he fell in the gutter where he went to sleep. It should be remembered that undertakers used to go round the city in the night and pick up the dead from the streets to take them to the mass graves outside the city walls. The drunken Augustin was mistaken for a dead man, picked up and dumped in the nearest mass grave. But Augustin wasn't dead, so he was very shocked when he woke up and found himself among all the corpses. As the grave was very deep and the walls too high for him to climb out himself, he started to play his bag pipes as loud as he could to attract the attention of the undertakers when they came round to dump another load of corpses. Luckily, the next undertaker heard him playing and was very surprised to find someone still alive and shouting for help. He was immediately rescued from this dreadful place and was very lucky to remain healthy despite his terrible close contact with the disease. He then told people in his songs about his dreadful experience and they loved him all the more for that. We still all know how to sing his song: "Oh, du lieber Augustin alles hin, Geld is hin, Mensch is hin, oh, du lieber Augustin, alles is hin". (Which goes like this: "Oh , you dear Augustin, all is gone, money is gone, man is gone, oh, dear Augustin, all is gone").

Leaving the ancient inn and our bag piper we continue along the street of the meat trade the **Fleischmarkt,** past the main post office and then take two right turns to bring us into **Schönlaterngasse (Beautiful Lamp Lane).** The small winding lane got its name from a beautiful wrought iron lamp, which might have been made in the old smithy there but is now at the **Historisches Museum der Stadt Wien** (History Museum of Vienna, on Karlsplatz next to Karlskirche) where it can be seen together with many other old house signs, pictures, suits of armour, furniture and costumes of the Biedermeier and Baroque era, and even showing a large model of the Medieval city with its city walls around it.

The inn called **Alte Schmiede (Old Smithy)** is still decorated with a skilfully made wrought iron key. Inside we can see the old workshop of a locksmith, his tools, anvil and furnace, as well as locks and lamps.

The house just next to the **Old Smithy,** is called **"Zum Basilisken" (The Basilisk)** a mythological lizard type beast that was supposedly a cross-breeding of a cock, a toad and a snake. It tells us in a picture painted on the house wall, the story of a brave baker who killed such a poisonous beast. The basilisk, here made of sandstone, is sitting in a niche above the painting. According to legend the basilisk was found in the well of a bakery.

The "Basilisk" at the bakery.

THE BASILISK AT THE BAKERY

The bakery in Schönlaterngasse was well known for its good bread. The Master baker and his helpers started baking in the early morning hours every day so as to have fresh bread and rolls ready for their customers at breakfast time. Even the young house maid had to start early and fetch water from the well for the bakery, before she started any other house work. One day the maid noticed a terrible smell coming from the well. This was so bad that she became too sick to pull the bucket up, and she was only able to shout for help before falling unconscious. The baker and his apprentices went to see what was going on and saved her, but couldn't see the reason for the smell as it was too repulsive. Only one of them was brave enough to go near the well and climb down into it, but after only one minute he had to be pulled out again. The shouting and crying in the bakery had attracted the attention of many people who wanted to know what was going on. The poor baker could only tell them that there was a strange looking creature in the well, which had the head of a cock with a golden crown on it, the body of a toad and the tail of a snake and a terrible stare in his eyes. Nobody knew what to do except the emperor's doctor, who was a well educated man and had read of similar creatures in Greek mythology. He proposed that somebody must go down into the well with a mirror to scare the creature so much with its own nasty appearance that it would die of shock due to its own ugliness. But he warned them still to be very careful, because from his knowledge any-body who had ever seen such a beast before, had always died. Georg, one of the baker's helpers, who was secretly in love with the maid, volunteered to undertake this task to gain the Master's approval of their marriage plan. With the Master's agreement the doctor prepared Georg well; he blind-folded him so that he couldn't see the creature, sealed his ears with wax so that he could not hear the monster, covered his nose with the maid's scarf; gave him a mirror and led him to the well, where he fixed a rope round his body to be able to pull him up again. Georg climbed down into the well, holding the mirror in front of himself just like his name-sake Saint George had held his shield to protect him in his fight with the dragon. Down in the well the basilisk looked into the mirror and saw for the first time just how ugly he really was. This experience frightened him so much that he burst with an enormous bang releasing an even more repulsive smell. The doctor and his helpers pulled Georg up quickly. Even though he was ill for some time he survived this dangerous adventure because of the doctor's wise precautions and care. The well was filled in with stones to prevent people using water from this contaminated well in future. Only the painting on the house wall reminds us of the brave young man who killed the monster with a mirror.

At the corner of Schönlaterngasse we can walk through the courtyard of the Heiligenkreuzer Hof monastery and via Fleischmarkt will get back to **Rotenturm Straße (Red Tower Street).** Here we can still see the picture of the Red Tower, painted on a house wall, that gave the street its name; however the oil painting of the Red Tower at the History Museum of Vienna, gives us a much better idea of what it looked like.

Vienna protected by city walls and the Red Tower in 1700, by Delsenbach- "Historisches Museum Wien"

THE RED TOWER

According to legend, the Red Tower gate house was a very busy entrance used by many people going in or out of the medieval city. There was a strange piece of wood fixed above the portcullis of this gate, which looked like a rasher of bacon with a little verse written on it as follows:

"If there is a man, who can truly claim that he isn't under his wife's thumb, he shall be able to take the bacon off the tower."

Although everyone disliked it, nobody dared to attempt to remove it. One day however, a man appeared before the town council claiming that he was the true master of his house and that he could therefore remove this insulting board for them and the town council gave him permission to try. Of course, it soon got round that a man was going to remove the board and many people gathered at the Red Tower to watch. A ladder was brought and this man started to climb the steps. Half way up the ladder he suddenly stopped and then climbed down again. Turning towards the watching crowd he declared. "Someone else has to go up first and clean the bacon before I touch it because it is very dirty. Otherwise I would ruin my best suit and my wife would scold me for doing that." At first the crowd fell silent in surprise, but then a storm of laughter broke out. This self declared "hero" realised his foolishness and vanished quickly.

This board remained on the tower for many more years until finally the Red Tower was demolished, pleasing all the Viennese men who were very glad to see the back of this insulting piece of wood.

The street itself will take us back to our starting point on **Stephansplatz.**

From here a short walk down Singerstraße will take us to **Blutgasse (Blood Lane).** In Medieval times a large number of monks were brutally slaughtered in their monastery here and it was said that their blood ran down the little lane like a stream. Hence the name of the lane that takes us to Domgasse (Church Lane) where the courageous Polish street trader Kolschitzky opened the first ever coffee house in Vienna.

When you are enjoying a cup of coffee next time in one of Vienna's coffee houses, remember that Viennese coffee was not introduced to us by an Italian or Greek (who are world famous for their strong coffee), but by a Polish street trader. He showed the Viennese how to prepare and enjoy coffee made from Turkish coffee beans left behind after the Turkish siege of Vienna in 1683, which leads us to another legend.

Relief of Vienna from the Turkish siege 1683
(by Geffels - "Historisches Museum Wien")

KOLSCHITZKY'S COFFEE BEANS

The Polish street trader Kolschitzky had been living in Vienna for several years, when the second Turkish siege began in early 1683. He had previously spent several years travelling in Turkey, so he knew their customs, traditions and language very well. At the peak of the Turkish siege he offered to help the defending commander of Vienna, Graf Starhemberg, by smuggling a message through the Turkish lines to find out when the relief army would finally come. Graf Starhemberg accepted the offer gratefully, since he hoped that someone who spoke Turkish would be more successful than all others who had already tried and failed. Those who had been caught by the Turks were hanged near the city walls as a deterrent and also to demoralise the population. Graf Starhemberg gave Kolschitzky and his accompanying servant a letter for the commander of the relief army and accompanied them to the city gate Schottentor, from where they had to try to get through the Turkish occupied area and reach the relief army gathering somewhere further up the Danube.

On their way through the Turkish camp Kolschitzky and his servant wore Turkish clothes and spoke only Turkish so that they wouldn't be easily recognised. Despite that a Turkish soldier became suspicious of them and brought them before his commander.

Questioned by the commander, Kolschitzky said that he was in fact a trader from Belgrade, travelling with the Turkish army selling food to the soldiers. The commander believed him and even warned him not to get to close to the Christians, who might kill him. So Kolschitzky was freed to continue on his way. The two men made their way carefully towards the little village of Kahlenberg near the Danube north of Vienna where they approached some local people to help them cross the river. First they were shot at, as they were still wearing their Turkish clothes and mistaken for Turkish soldiers. Only when they shouted their request loudly in German, were they taken across the river to the commander of the Emperor's relief army, Count Lothringen. The Austrian commander assured them that a relief army made up of the Emperor's troops together with Polish troops was being formed and would be ready for the fight for Vienna within a few weeks. Kolschitzky and his servant were told to have a good rest that night so as to be ready to take the commander's reply back to Graf Starhemberg the following day.

However, Kolschitzky had one request before retiring for the night, namely that a rocket should be launched as a signal to Vienna that he had succeeded in reaching the relief troops. This request was fulfilled and soon afterwards an acknowledgement rocket was fired from St. Stephan's Cathedral. Now Kolschitzky was satisfied and went to sleep. Early next morning he returned safely to Vienna.

On September 11th 1683 at midnight the troops of the relief army gathered together on the hills of Kahlenberg and Leopoldsberg. They were blessed in an outdoor mass celebrated in their camp by the Polish capuchin monk Marc Avian, who accompanied the Polish King Jan Sobieski.

At sunrise next day the relief troops charged downhill and made a surprise attack on the Turkish camp. By late afternoon, the Turkish army had fled in panic leaving all their goods behind them.

The Viennese and their liberators were overjoyed with the relief of Vienna. Emperor Leopold I awarded both the courageous liberators and the defenders of Vienna with generous gifts. When Kolschitzky was asked what he would like to receive for his brave deed, he said that he would be content just to have the many sacks of 'green beans' that the Turks had left behind. The Emperor said that he had also heard about those beans, but nobody knew what use they had. So Kolschitzky explained to him that the Turks made their favourite drink, "black coffee" from them. He also knew how to make this drink and would like to introduce it to the Viennese if he was granted the coffee beans and given a house to sell it from. In the beginning the Viennese didn't like that black bitter brew, but eventually got used to it and more and more people came to

Kolschitzky's coffee house. Even Graf Starhemberg and the young French soldier Eugene of Savoy (later to become the famous Prince Eugene), who had fought courageously under Count Lothringen in the relief army, came regularly for a cup of coffee and a chat about their military adventures.

From Kolschitzky's remembrance place in the little Domgasse, it is only a short walk to **Prince Eugene's** palace in Himmelpfortgasse. To get there, walk down Singerstraße; turn right into Seilerstätte and continue on past the **"British Bookshop"** in Weihburggasse until the corner with Himmelpfortgasse, where the **City Palace of Prince Eugene** (now used by the Ministry of Finance) is located.

Crown of the House of Habsburg

The golden crowns of the House of Babenberg and the House of Habsburg above the two entrances indicate the significance of its former owners. As a result of his success in the relief of Vienna the young French noble-man, **Eugene of Savoy,** was given the title **Prince** and promoted to be commander of the Emperor's troops. He fought many wars for the Austrian Emperor over the next 50 years, including more battles against the Turkish army, which was still occupying Hungary and Yugoslavia. The Prince and his troops freed Budapest from the Turks following an occupation of about 150 years and brought the Hungarian realm back under the House of Habsburg. This was his greatest success.

Between his battles on the different fronts in the East and the West of Europe he lived in the **Stadt Palais (City Palace).**

Prince Eugene of Savoy was also a dedicated man of the arts. He collected many sculptures, paintings and books. His book collection is now displayed at the Nationalbibliothek (National Library) on Josefsplatz. Since he was very important to the Emperor, he was even allowed to build his own summer palace called the **BELVEDERE** on the sloping hills outside the city walls, between Rennweg and Prince Eugene Straße. A fifteen minutes walk will take us there.

BELVEDERE - PALACES

STARTING POINT
U1, U2, U4 Karlsplatz
Tram D and 71

UNTERES BELVEDERE: Rennweg 6a
OBERES BELVEDERE: Prinz Eugen Straße 27

The **Belvedere - Palaces** (built between 1700 and 1724) consist of two Baroque palaces: the **Untere (lower) Belvedere** and the **Obere (upper) Belvedere**, which are linked by a beautifully terraced garden with several fountains on different levels.

Both palaces are now used as Museums of Art and display a large variety of Austrian paintings from the Middle Ages up to the 20th Century, including well known painters like Gustav Klimt, Oskar Kokoschka and Egon Schiele in addition to Prince Eugene's own collection. Paintings of his great war victories are shown in the Marble Hall of the **Untere Belvedere.**

The **Obere Belvedere** was the setting for one of the most important events of today's Austrian Republic. On May 15th 1955 the Foreign Ministers of France, Great Britain, Russia, the United States and Austria signed the Austrian State Treaty restoring Austria's independence following a 10 year occupation after the Second World War. The Marble Hall of the Obere

Belvedere has since been dedicated to that event. One large painting shows the foreign ministers signing the treaty. Another picture depicts the moment when the Austrian foreign minister Leopold Figl showed the signed treaty to the crowd and exclaimed these famous words: "Österreich ist frei!" (Austria is free!).

The palace of the Obere Belvedere actually stands on a hill from where we have a wonderful view over the gardens as well as the city, which seems to spread out from the end of the garden right up to the hills of the Vienna Woods. In the distance we can make out the little church on Leopoldsberg from where Prince Eugene looked at the city before the relief battle.

Belvedere-Palaces

KINGS AND QUEENS OF AUSTRIA

STARTING POINT
U1, U3 Stephansplatz / City
via Graben to Am Hof

As many street names remind us of certain trades, like: Goldschmiedgasse (Gold-smith's Lane), Kohlmarkt (Coal Market), Tuchlauben (Textile Arcade) or Färberstraße (Dyer's Street), so are others dedicated to former kings and queens of Austria like: **Maria-Theresien-Staße, Elisabethstraße, Franz-Josefs-Kai** reminding us of the Habsburger Dynasty; as well as **Jasomirgottstraße** (just opposite St. Stephan's Cathedral), **Babenbergerstraße,** and **Am Hof** (the site of the former Babenberger castle) are reminders of the Babenberger Dynasty ruling Austria from 976 to 1246.

THE BABENBERGER COURT - AM HOF

Am Hof (At the Court) the square that used to be the court yard of the Babenberger castle in the 12th century. Unfortunately there is nothing left of it nowadays, except the beautifully laid out square where the knights held tournaments practising in their heavy armour both on foot and on horseback. Here they also celebrated feasts for visiting knights who were travelling through Vienna on their way to fight in the Crusades. An important part of such feasts was the entertainment by ballad singers with their songs and stories. One of these stories is told in the following legend.

Babenberger knights at a tournament

A CHRISTMAS SURPRISE FOR THE DUKE

abenberger knights had originally come from Augsburg, Germany, so it was not surprising that they invited tradesmen, clergymen and even mint-masters from there. However, they also invited many from other countries such as Belgium, that also had connections to their court. They gave them the right to open businesses here and even granted them citizenship, which upset the Viennese tradesmen. They were especially worried that the Belgian mint-masters were allowed to mint the Viennese coins and had so become Duke Leopold's money makers. Those who had lent money to the Duke before, were now afraid that they would never get their money back from the Duke and so thought up a plan to try and solve this problem. They were fully convinced that the Duke would help them to get back into business, if only he could be made to fully appreciate their situation.

It was just before Christmas when the eldest member of the town council Master Pippin learned that the Duke was going to ride through the streets of Vienna on Christmas Eve. He quickly called a meeting of the town council at the old town hall, outlined his plan to them and when everybody agreed, they hurried to organise everything for his Christmas Eve surprise.

It was a truly beautiful Christmas Eve and the city was covered with fresh snow and the people had decorated their houses nicely. When night had fallen Duke Leopold and his most trusted friend mounted their horses and left the castle to enjoy the beautiful evening on a ride through Vienna. The city was very quiet with only house lights shining, so what a surprise they had when they arrived at Stephansplatz. The square was full of people waiting for the Duke, holding candles to light up the dark night and warm their freezing hands and faces. As soon as the Duke appeared the crowd broke out in loud cheering, which only stopped when old Pippin stepped forward to wish the Duke a Merry Christmas. He asked the Duke to accept the gifts his people had brought as a little thank you for all his care and kindness. The Duke was overwhelmed by the sight of the thousands of people waiting with gifts for him and so thanked them for this sign of love. In gratitude he asked, if they had any wish that he could grant them in return. This was the moment old Pippin had been waiting for. He was now able to tell the Duke how much they were worried about losing the money they had lent to the knights of his court and asked him to help them to get their loans back. The Duke agreed and asked them to come to the castle the very next day to put forward their demands in writing so that he could help them. Pippin thanked the Duke for this gesture and then the people formed a long procession to bring their gifts to the Duke's castle.

Not far from **Am Hof,** just down **Heidenschuss** and across the **Tiefer Graben** we are at the **Freyung,** where we see on the side wall of the **Schottenkirche** a more than life size statue of the Babenberger Duke Heinrich II "Jasomirgott".

Duke Heinrich Jasomirgott at the Scot's Church

 He got his nickname of "Jasomirgott" because whenever he started a big task, he would always say: "Ja, so mir Gott helfe", which means: "Yes, so help me God". It was he who moved the royal court to Vienna from the Leopoldsberg and the residence at Klosterneuburg.

Duke Heinrich was a very religious man (like his father Leopold III the "Saint") who not only started the reconstruction of St. Stephan's Cathedral, but also invited the Irish Benedictine monks from Regensburg to his city and built them the Schottenkirche, church and monastery. At that time Ireland was called "New Scotland" and their church was therefore called the Scots Church, even though it was founded by Irish Benedictine monks. In those days the church was also a place of refuge for persecuted people, and it was said that anybody who reached the walls of the monastery was given sanctuary and was in safety. This is where the old German name for this square **Freyung (to be freed)** comes from.

When the **Babenberger** rulers originally came in 976, they were given the Eastern borderlands of the Holy Roman Empire, on condition they governed and defended these territories in the EAST against invading tribes. They gradually fought their way eastwards along the Danube to re-take control of these territories from the invading troops of Huns, Slavs, Avars. In doing so they built numerous monasteries and fortified castles, such as: **Pöchlarn, Melk, Göttweig, Tulln, Klosterneuburg, Leopoldsberg** and further along the Danube. Austria's Latin name "Ostarichi" (now Österreich) comes from the reference to its location in the Eastern part of the Holy Roman Empire of German Nation. The name Ostarichi was first mentioned in a gift certificate to the town Neuhofen/Ybbs in Lower Austria in 996. The Babenbergers were also dedicated Christians, who followed the call of the church to defend Christianity in the Crusades. It is said that it was at a battle during the Crusades where the colours **RED - WHITE - RED** of the Austrian flag were established.

According to legend during one of the Crusades in the Holy Land Duke Leopold V was severely wounded in a fierce battle. During the battle blood from his wounds soaked his long white coat from collar to hem turning it totally red. Only when he took off his belt after the battle did he notice that there was an unspoilt white stripe left in the middle. From then on he decided to use the colours RED - WHITE - RED as the colour of Austria's flag.

It was also at the battle in Akron that he had a dispute with King Richard the Lion-heart, which lead to the imprisonment of this English King at castle Dürnstein a few years later.

RICHARD THE LION-HEART

About 800 years ago Emperor Barbarossa of Germany lead a large multinational-national Christian army on a Crusade to the Holy Land to free Christian cities from their pagan rulers. This army included troops of King Richard the Lion-heart of England and the Austrian Duke Leopold V in addition to French, German and numerous others.

After the death of Emperor Barbarossa during the Crusade a big dispute developed as to who should take over command, which grew into a major quarrel between King Richard and Duke Leopold. In 1191 at the end of the siege of Akron the Austrian Duke had his newly created red - white - red flag raised on the city ramparts as a sign of an Austrian victory.

However, this angered his ally King Richard, who's army had also fought in the battle. In anger he had the Austrian flag hauled down and thrown into the mud of the battle field, which annoyed the Austrian Duke so much that he and his army immediately left the Holy Land. Since many other parts of the army left as well, the English King and his army were soon left on their own.

However, he could not continue the fight against the huge number of enemies on his own and therefore had to return to Europe.

Although most of the crusaders travelled back home over land, King Richard and his army sailed back so as to avoid travelling through the countries belonging to his newly acquired "enemy" the Austrian Duke.

Unfortunately the king's ship sank in a storm and forcing him to travel over land with his few remaining followers. They dressed themselves in the clothes of poor pilgrims, hoping that nobody would recognise them, and tried to get through Austria as quickly as possible. However, just before Christmas in 1192 cold winter weather and hunger forced them to ask for shelter and food at a village inn near Vienna. King Richard disguised as a pilgrim, was told to cook his own meal in the kitchen which he and his followers did. Unfortunately while preparing their food an old Austrian crusader noticed that one of the "poor pilgrims" was wearing a precious ring and guessed immediately that this could well be the King of England who he had seen in the Holy Land. The soldier reported his discovery and soon the Duke's soldiers came and arrested King Richard. They brought him first before the Duke at the castle in Vienna, but since this place did not seem safe enough to hold such a famous prisoner, the Duke moved the King to the fortified castle at Dürnstein.

The story of the King's ship sinking reached England and many people thought the King had actually died. The King's brother John pronounced himself the new

King of England. However, King Richard's former minstrel Blondel was not convinced that his King had died and set out to search for news of him, taking his harp and travelling Eastwards along the Rhine and the Danube. Suspecting that Richard had maybe been captured and imprisoned, he sang at each castle the song that only he and Richard knew, in the hope of getting a reply from him. Finally he came as far as Dürnstein on the Danube, where he started to sing their favourite song outside the castle. When he had finished the first verse and stopped singing, he suddenly heard a voice in the distance continuing the song. This was wonderful news for Blondel, who now knew definitely that Richard was still alive and where he was imprisoned. He found out that King Richard could be released on payment of a large ransom and immediately returned to England to tell the people that King Richard was still alive.

In spring 1193 King Richard was finally released and returned home after payment of the ransom.

The Austrian Duke used the huge ransom sum to enlarge and strengthen the fortification walls around Vienna, which protected the city for many centuries against all sorts of invaders, including the Turkish sieges in 1529 and 1683.

It is said, that although most of this legend is historically true, the part about Blondel's unshakeable faithfulness and loyalty has been added for romantic reasons. The walls of the castle in the little village Dürnstein in the Wachau area of the Danube (80 km west from Vienna) may be crumbling, but the memory of the truly loved and admired King Richard still lives on today.

Another reminder of the Crusades is the Gothic cross on Triesterstraße in the 10th district, made by Master Hans Puchsbaum, which is called: **Spinnerin am Kreuz (Spinner at the Cross)** and is made of white sand-stone like St. Stephan's Cathedral.

Gothic cross called: "Spinnerin am Kreuz"

THE CRUSADER'S FAITHFUL WIFE

Long before the stone cross was made, a simple wooden cross stood at the top of the Wiener-berg. From here one could see St. Stephan's Cathedral in the city on the one side and far into the countryside to the south.

It was the last place of farewell for the Crusaders on their way to the Holy Land to fight with Duke Leopold of Austria. Among those saying farewell was a young woman who had tried desperately to persuade her newly wed husband to stay with her rather than join the Crusade. However, this knight was determined to go and so she promised to wait for him faithfully and would have a stone cross erected in place of the old wooden one when he came back to her safe and sound. To give her vow more meaning, she decided to earn the money for the new cross with her own bare hands. Every day she took her spinning wheel to the wooden cross at the top of the Wienerberg to work while she was waiting for her beloved husband. She soon became a well known figure there and was able to sell all the cloth and wool she made, which helped her in her effort.

After a year, some of the knights started to return from the Crusade and eventually even Duke Leopold with the bulk of his army, but not the wife's husband.

Unfortunately she had to wait for him much longer

than all the other families who had to let their beloved men go to the war, but she was still convinced that he would return. After several years of waiting finally one day the woman noticed a very poorly dressed and tired man walking up the hill towards the cross. At first she didn't even think that it could be her husband, but when she looked closely at him, she recognised the family ring on his finger and couldn't hold back any longer: "It's you, you have finally come home! I knew it, I never gave up hope that you would come back, and now you are here!" At first the man also didn't recognise his wife, especially as he had definitely not expected to meet her at the cross where they had parted so long ago. After embracing each other passionately he finally told her of his terrible experiences in the Crusade. He had only taken part in one battle when he was wounded and caught by the enemies who kept him as a slave. Luckily he finally managed to escape from slavery and found his way back home.

Thankful for her husband's return, the woman immediately fulfilled her vow by having the wooden cross replaced by a beautiful stone cross.

With that legend of the Crusades we will leave the Babenberger Dynasty for a while and look at some stories related to the House of Habsburg.

The Imperial Palace: Hofburg

THE HABSBURG COURT AT THE HOFBURG

STARTING POINT
U1, U3 Stephansplatz / City
via Graben and Kohlmarkt to Michaelerplatz

The **Hofburg (Imperial Palace)** was the seat of all reigning monarchs of the House of Habsburg from its very beginning in 1276 up to 1918 when the monarchy was dissolved and Austria declared a republic. Even today the Presidents of Austria use those parts of the Hofburg which overlook the Heldenplatz and the Ballhausplatz, where the Austrian Government has its seat. When the President is in the Hofburg the Austrian flag is raised on the top of the roof and since Austria joined the European Union, the blue European flag with its yellow stars flies next to the red-white-red Austrian flag.

In a guided tour you can see some of the splendid rooms of the former emperors, which give a vivid picture of their life style during the different centuries. Each of the long list of Habsburg monarchs had his own rooms and wings added to the already existing buildings on being crowned king. As a result the Hofburg now consists of 18 wings, 19 court-yards and about 2600 rooms. All of them are still in use but mostly as conference rooms, museums or ball rooms for special occasions.

There are several museums in the **Neue Hofburg** in which you can see, for instance, the arms and suits of armour of the Babenberger knights, as well as furniture and musical instruments of later periods. Exhibits from excavations in foreign countries like Ephesus in Turkey or special exhibitions from Mexico, Africa and many other countries can be seen at the **Museum of Ethnology.**

The **Nationalbibliothek (National Library)** on Josefsplatz has a collection of more than 2 million books and maps collected by members of the former Austrian royal families, Prince Eugene of Savoy and later the State of Austria.

At the other end of Josefsplatz you find the Winter Riding School where the famous white **Lipizzaner Horses of the Spanish Riding School** perform. If you wait at the door to the stables in Reitschulgasse 2 you might catch a glimpse of the horses on their way through the court yard to and fro from the Winter Riding School. However, an even better chance to see them is guaranteed by visiting the Lipizzaner Museum.

The oldest part of the Hofburg is the **Schweizer Hof (Swiss Court)** with its massive gate house, the **Schweizer Tor (Swiss Gate),** where you can see parts of the former castle moat and chain bridge that belonged to the original building, a Burg (castle) dating back to 1279. The Schweizer Tor, was reconstructed in

Renaissance style in 1552 and got its name from Empress Maria Theresia who had Swiss soldiers standing guard at her palace. When you walk through the **Schweizer Tor** into the court-yard, look up at the ceiling, which is painted with the red-white-red coat of arms of the Babenberger Dukes.

The Swiss Gate

Inside the **Schweizer Hof** you can see the **Crown Jewels** of the Babenberger and Habsburg kings and queens at the Treasury. This is located underneath the stairs to the entrance to the Palace Chapel, where the Vienna Boys Choir sings at Sunday mass. If you stand in the middle of the Schweizer Hof and imagine a tower at each corner you can get an impression of how small the original castle was when the first Habsburger family moved into it in 1276.

COUNT RUDOLPH OF HABSBURG

Rudolph of Habsburg, whose father's castle the Habsburg was in Switzerland, was crowned "German King" in Aachen, with instructions to restore law and order in the south eastern part of the Holy Roman Empire, which is now Austria. This he did and defeated King Ottokar Premysl of Bohemia, who had captured Austria after the Babenberger dynasty had died out. The victory over the Bohemian King confirmed and strengthened Rudolph's role as a Germanic King and he was rewarded by being given these lands where he established a dynasty that ruled for more than 600 years. The Habsburgs had to fight many wars to keep their empire together, but to extend it to the massive size it reached at its height, they adhered to their motto: "Let others wage war for a throne - you, happy Austria, marry". Habsburg children were married to the children of the Kings and Queens of Burgundy, Italy, Spain, Bohemia and so on and inherited in due time all of those countries. At its peak King Charles V could boast to rule over an Empire "on which the sun never set", being the ruler of territories that reached from Bulgaria on the Black Sea to Spain on the Atlantic Ocean, as well as its colonies in Mexico. Not all of the Habsburgs however, were happy or successful in their roles. Poor Marie-Antoinette, for instance, married to the French King Louis VI by her mother Empress Maria Theresia in 1770, was beheaded 23 years later during the French revolution in 1793.

EMPRESS MARIA THERESIA
...and her advisors, on Maria Theresien-Platz

The most famous and beloved monarch was **Empress Maria Theresia.** In order to continue the Habsburg line, her father Emperor Karl VI who had no male heir, promised her hand in marriage to the Duke of Lothringen at the age of four years. When they were finally married 15 years later and her father died, Maria Theresia however, decided to succeed to the throne herself and ruled the country from 1740 to 1780. It was very difficult for her to keep Austria's strong position among the other European countries as she was considered a weak woman who could be robbed easily of her territories. However, with the help of her husband, her advisors and loyal subjects she succeeded in fighting off all advances on her territories. Most important to her however, was her beloved husband Franz Stephan and their 16 children. Although she loved them dearly, she made them spend many hours studying, even more hours praying in church, as well as practising music and acting in plays. She even had a theatre built for them. The little princes and princesses were immensely impressed by the six-year old **Wolfgang Amadeus Mozart** who played the piano for the Empress on a visit to Schönbrunn Palace one day. The young artist was so overwhelmed by the Empress that he jumped on her lap and embraced and kissed her after he had finished his performance. He was also taken by the little princesses and even proposed marriage to one of them. Although this was surprising behaviour, even for such a young visitor, the Empress took no offence and sent him a present a few days later. Maria Theresia was also convinced that it was her duty to look after her young subjects as she looked after her own children. It disturbed her immensely that most children could neither read nor write, and so she introduced free schooling for all children from the age of six to fourteen. This meant that not only the children of rich people be educated, but also the poor had a chance to improve their lives. Many of the other reforms proposed during her reign were put into force later, by her son Emperor Joseph II.

EMPEROR JOSEPH II

Emperor Joseph II in front of the National Library

He maintained a close contact to his subjects during his reign and is still known as the people's emperor who wanted the best for all of them. However at his time, his ideas weren't appreciated as they were too modern for his people. It was under his reign that the vast imperial hunting ground the **Prater** was changed to a public recreation area; and the first **General Hospital** was opened for sick and needy people. His sense of justice and charity are told in many legends.

THE EMPEROR ON THE MARKET

The emperor happened to hear that eggs were being sold at an unusually high price and so he put on civilian clothes and went to the local market to enquire himself. When told the price the emperor exclaimed that this was terribly expensive, but bought two eggs anyway. After some time he returned to the same stall and asked if he had any more eggs to sell, as he wanted to buy them all. The surprised trader wanted to know why he would now buy all of them, if he considered them to be too expensive. The emperor replied that he had found a piece of gold in each egg when he had cracked them open. "Oh, this I can do myself", the trader exclaimed and started to crack open all of his eggs but unfortunately for him didn't find any gold. The emperor, who had taught him a lesson for life, disappeared quickly and the price of eggs went down again.

THE EMPEROR HELPS A POOR FAMILY
One day the emperor saw a little boy crying and begging in the street. When he asked him why he was

crying, the boy told him that he was supposed to fetch a doctor for his sick mother, but the doctor refused to come because he could not pay in advance. The emperor took pity on him, gave him a gold ducat and asked him for his home address. While the boy ran away happily to fetch the doctor, the emperor went to the boy's home and enquired about the poor woman's health. He then gave her a written note and left the house. When the boy arrived with the doctor, the woman was surprised that a second doctor was now coming to see her and showed the real doctor the note she had been given by the first one. The doctor read what she believed to be a prescription and exclaimed: "The Emperor visited you! This note entitles you to 25 gold ducats!" The woman was of course, very happy about this generous gift. This made the doctor however, feel extremely ashamed about his initial reaction and he promised to himself to be more generous in future.

THE EMPEROR AND THE HERDSMAN

As a young man, the emperor travelled from castle to castle to get to know his country and his people. Above the doorway of one castle he saw a motto stating: "We know no worries!", which he found most interesting. He asked the knights living in the castle if it was true that they knew no worries, while he, emperor of the whole country, knew nothing but worries. They confirmed that the motto was correct but could not explain why. In order to find out how they did it, he asked them the following three questions to be answered by the time he returned in three days.

"How deep is the sea? How long does it take to travel to heaven? How far apart is happiness from unhappiness?" Over the next days the knights of the castle tried to find suitable answers to these questions, but they couldn't. The priest of the castle chapel, who was a very educated man, also didn't know any suitable answers.

In desperation they even asked their herdsman, who happened to pass by with his animals. To their surprise he actually thought that the questions were very easy to answer. In order not to embarrass themselves, they dressed the herdsman in the priest's clothes and told him to give his answers to the emperor. When the big moment came and the emperor asked for the answers to his questions, the herdsman stepped forward and said:

"The sea is a stone's throw deep. It takes only a day to reach heaven, because there is only one Ascension Day. Happiness is very close to unhappiness, because today I stand as a priest in front of you whereas yesterday I was only a lowly herdsman."

The emperor was so impressed by these answers that he

told the knights to raise the herdsman's living standard to that of a priest from now on.

THE ROYAL GUIDE

Maria Theresia had the palace at Schönbrunn renovated according to her family's needs and wishes, she even included a zoo where exotic animals were kept in cages. She particularly loved to have breakfast with her husband at the little pavilion in the middle of the zoo while watching the animals around them. The later Emperor Franz I however, was more fond of the extensive gardens around the palace and also liked to do some gardening himself. One day after a large number of unusual animals had been added to the zoo collection, a group of guests came to visit. Among them was an army general who unfortunately lost his way in the extensive gardens. Seeing somebody working on a flower bed, he asked him the way back to the zoo and even offered him a gold coin if the "gardener" would take him there. The "gardener" kindly agreed and started to walk with the visitor towards the zoo. Suddenly the general recognised the emperor (despite him wearing such common clothes) and started to apologise desperately. However, the emperor just said: "Never mind, I will gladly still show you the way, but you can't have your money back, as this is the first money that these animals have ever earned me."

FRANZ JOSEPH I AND ELISABETH I

Empress Elisabeth I and Emperor Franz Joseph I

Emperor Franz Joseph I and his beloved wife Empress Elisabeth, the last monarchs to rule over the Austrian empire from 1848 to 1916, still have a special place in the hearts of the Viennese. They are thought of with love and admiration, but also sadness due to their unhappy life, which was more often spent separated than together.

When Emperor Franz Joseph was in his early twenties his mother, Archduchess Sophie, decided that it was time for him to marry because the empire needed a male heir to continue the dynasty. Therefore she made an arrangement for him to meet Princess Helene of Wittelsbach during a family gathering at their summer residence in Bad Ischl. However, Franz Joseph fell in love with Helene's younger sister Elisabeth instead.

Images of Empress Elisabeth I throughout her life.

Elisabeth, who was only 16 years old and called Sissi by her brothers and sisters. She had only been taken along as a companion for her elder sister and was completely unprepared for such a royal association. She had not been educated to become a queen like her elder sister and lived a natural and unrestricted life of a child growing up in the country with animals and horses, enjoying riding in particular. Falling in love with the Emperor of Austria however, meant that she had to leave her beloved home at Possenhof at the Starhembergersee in Bavaria. Within a few months Sissi had to learn French, Italian and Austrian history, as well as court ceremony, before she could travel to Vienna to marry the Emperor. On her journey down the Danube she was greeted everywhere with enthusiasm, but was already exhausted when she was greeted by the Emperor on her arrival in Vienna.

However, this was only the beginning; the introduction to the royal court and the wedding ceremony took several days. Poor Sissi was so overwhelmed that she broke down in tears and fled the banquet room on the last day. Unfortunately the Emperor had very little time to spend together with her during their honeymoon at the palace in Laxenburg, because he had to return to his duties in Vienna every day. Sissi had to get used to having many strange people around her and to the very strict protocol her mother-in-law, Archduchess Sophie, insisted upon. This did not even change when Sissi had her first child. The Archduchess even arranged that the nursery for the baby had to be near her rooms and also employed nannies to look after it. The nursery was far away from Sissi's rooms and she always had to ask permission first before she could see her own child. This made her very sad and also angry with her husband because he would not help her in this dispute with his mother. This did not even change by the time Sissi had her third child, a boy. The only times when she could be free of her mother-in-law's strict protocol and happy together with her husband, were during their many trips to get to know the Empire. Sissi particularly loved Hungary of all the countries of the Austrian Empire. The Hungarian nobility and politicians also loved her. She even learned to speak Hungarian to be able to understand them. This impressed the Hungarians very much and made it possible for her to mediate in disputes between them and her husband. Soon the Hungarians were convinced that all good things came from Sissi and all bad things came from the Archduchess Sophie, who hated them for their resistance against Austrian rule. Meanwhile Sissi often became very ill and when she got pneumonia doctors recommended that she be sent away for a while to a warm climate. From that time on she travelled often and spent less and less time at court with her husband. Only when Hungarian matters developed to crisis levels would she return to influence her husband in favour of the Hungarians.

This resulted in her greatest success when in 1867 the Austro-Hungarian Empire was formed with Emperor Franz Joseph and Empress Elisabeth as king and queen of Hungary. From that time on Austria - Hungary was a double monarchy.

Emperor Franz Joseph I

The Hungarians however, were not the only problem for the Emperor, who was often at war on several fronts of his Empire. During all the 68 years of his reign Emperor Franz Joseph I spent most of his time trying to keep peace among the many different peoples of his empire. Although many tragic events over shadowed his life, (his son Crown Prince Rudolph shot himself; and his wife Sissi was assassinated), the Emperor did many good things for the country.

In particular, he was instrumental in drastically modernising the City of Vienna. Since the old medieval city walls were no longer an effective defence against modern weapons, the Emperor decided to remove the city walls completely and make way for a wide, impressive street around the inner city. In 1865 the new boulevard called Ringstraße was opened by the Emperor and today still characterises Vienna.

During his reign the Danube seriously flooded the city on a number of occasions causing a lot of damage and death among the inhabitants living near the river. As a result he arranged for flood regulation measures to be started to contain the great masses of flood water coming down from the mountains following severe winters.

We still enjoy the result of another great endeavour of his times; the fresh, clean drinking water coming from the mountains. Two pipelines were built to bring fresh mountain water to the city. The first one was built to bring water from the 2000 meter high mountains Rax and Schneeberg 100 km south of Vienna. The second one comes from even further away, the Hochschwab mountain 200 km west of Vienna. Since both areas are now protected nature reserves, where no industry is allowed and only very limited access for people is possible, the water is always clean and unpolluted for us to enjoy. The fountain on Schwarzenberplatz that sparkles at night in all the colours of the rainbow, from an icy white to a dark cold blue, was erected for the opening ceremony of the Vienna water supply line in 1873.

Emperor Franz Joseph I, who preferred Schönbrunn to the Hofburg, was the only Habsburg emperor to be born and die at the Palace of Schönbrunn.

If you want to visit **"Schloß Schönbrunn"** you'll need to allow an extra day for this large palace, its surrounding park with the large plam house and the historic zoo. You can go there by underground, tram or bus.

SCHÖNBRUNN PALACE

STARTING POINT
U 4, Schönbrunn
Bus 15A, Tram 10, 58

Schönbrunner Schloßstraße

The best starting point to see the palace and the park is through the impressive wrought iron main gate, where two huge stone obelisks topped with golden eagles stand guard. To the left of the **Palace Square** is the **Schönbrunn Theatre,** which was built for Empress Maria Theresia's children as their own theatre stage; and to the right we have the **Wagenburg (Carriage Museum)** where you can see the collection of coaches used by the Habsburgs for their various trips to Budapest, Venice, Munich etc., as well as the one used for state occasions such as weddings and funerals.

The name **Schönbrunn (Beautiful Fountain)** comes from the spring that provided the palace with wonderful fresh water right from its very early days as a small hunting lodge. This water tasted so good that the emperors had it delivered to their table at the palace and so Maria Theresia had a grotto-like building built over the spring to protect it. We can still see this Grotto in the palace garden today.

The original palace, which was built in 1683 after the Turkish siege of Vienna, was greatly altered and extended in 1744 by Empress Maria Theresia for her large family, as well as later on by Emperor Franz Joseph I. He had the palace modernised for his young wife, Empress Elisabeth I. At that time the palace was fitted with electric light, flushing toilets and a warm-air heating system. Imagine what a tremendous comfort it meant to be able to switch on electric light in these large rooms instead of straining to see by candle light; or to heat the rooms by hot air instead of having to keep all of the individual wood stoves in all the rooms continually fuelled with logs and coal.

Schönbrunn Palace

The Gloriette, that airy building at the top of the hill behind the palace, actually means "glory" and was erected in 1775 to commemorate the fallen soldiers from the Seven Year war between the armies of Empress Maria Theresia and the Emperor of Perusia. The original plan was to build a palace at the top of the hill as big as that of Versailles. However when it came to be built, there wasn't enough money for such a large palace and the emperor changed the plans to a smaller building at the foot of the hill, having to content himself with just a French garden design. Although the Gloriette has now been converted to incorporate a coffee house, one can still walk up the narrow stairs to the top, where you can enjoy a wonderful view over the palace, the park and Vienna.

Palm House of Schönbrunn

For those who love nature, a visit to the zoo and the nearby **Palmenhaus (Palm House)** with its collection of tropical plants is highly recommended.

The **Tiergarten Schönbrunn (the Zoo)** was founded by Emperor Maximilian almost 250 years ago and is the oldest zoo in Europe. It still has the layout of the original "Menagerie of wild animals", but has recently been extensively modernised to improve both the needs of the animals and their visibility to the visitors. A legend tells us the story of the very first exotic animal to arrive in Vienna:

VIENNA'S FIRST ELEPHANT

In April 1552 a Habsburg Prince returned to Vienna after having spent many years in Spain. The people of Vienna had heard about his impending return and were very curious to see him and his entourage, together with the numerous gifts he was said to be bringing with him from such far-away countries as India. They were gathering in their best clothes and waiting full of anticipation for the royal coaches to come along Kärntner Straße and Graben. Everybody was keen to have a place in the first row along the streets to get the best view. Suddenly fearful cries were heard from the crowd when people saw for the first time in their lives a huge grey monster walking on four pillar-like legs. Although this "monster" was heavily guarded by armed men, they still wanted to run away in panic, but there were so many people on the streets so that nobody could flee. Only a few doctors and educated men of the court knew that this animal was in fact an elephant. They managed to calm the people and told them that the elephant was actually a very peaceful animal that wouldn't do any harm. On the contrary, it was a very useful animal that was used in Asia and Africa to help the people in their daily lives. The elephant walked calmly along the street between its guards and in line with all the royal coaches.

Suddenly a piercing cry of a woman in deadly fear broke the silence. A child had slipped out of his mother's hand and been pushed in front of the elephant. However, the elephant took the child gently with its trunk and lifted it over the heads of the crowd back into the arms of the mother and then continued slowly on its way again. People broke out in loud cheers and clapped and applauded the elephant all the way to the Hofburg, where it was presented to the emperor.

The parents of the child were of course overjoyed by the happy outcome of this event and kept fond memories of the elephant.

The elephant, who was one of the first foreign animals for the kings menagerie, unfortunately did not survive for very long in the cold climate of central Europe and died in December 1553. The only reminder of this event still existing is a chair made out of its bones which is kept at the monastery of Kremsmünster.

Elephants at Schönbrunn Zoo

Nowadays most of the old zoo has been rebuilt and modernised. Some of the 750 different species, such as the elephants, the hippopotamus, birds, and the crocodiles have already been moved to modern cages that provide them with better living conditions and allow us a better view of the animals.

The pavilion at the centre of the zoo was actually built for the royal family to sit there and watch their "pets". You can sit down there too, enjoying a rest at the now Pavilion coffee house.

Leaving the zoo via the **Hietzinger Tor** will bring you back to modern Vienna again, where you can use the Underground U4 from the Hietzing station to take you back to the city within a few minutes.

RINGSTRASSE: A TOUR

STARTING POINT
U3 Stubentor
Tram 1 and 2

By 1850 it was considered that fortification walls were no longer an effective defence measure and Emperor Franz Joseph I gave orders for the Vienna walls to be demolished. These 8 meter high walls, together with the moat and a stretch of bare fields of no-man's land called the "Glacis" separated the surrounding villages from the city. By removing the fortifications, the city and the villages would together form a much larger capital city and make room for an impressive wide boulevard lined with grand state buildings and parks.

The demolition work and construction of this impressive tree-lined street and some of its accompanying buildings was completed after only 7 years of work and opened by the Emperor in 1865. For a long time after that, it was a favourite Sunday afternoon activity to enjoy a ride in a "Fiaker" round the Ring, or go for a walk with family and friends in the shade of the trees on the Ring. These times are long gone by, but the Ring has maintained its impressive imperial glory despite being a main traffic route around the city.

Tour of the Ring in a "Fiaker"

There are many different ways to take your tour around the 4 km long **Ringstraße.** For instance you could hire a "Fiaker" (a horse drawn carriage) on Heldenplatz or Stephansplatz and be taken round the Ring as in former times and have the sights explained to you by the coachman. The more sporty among you could go on a bicycle ride around the well marked shady bicycle lanes. You might also just walk around the Ringstraße, using the tram that goes round the Ring whenever you feel like having a rest. The tram lines 1 and 2 go all the way around the Ring (line 1 clockwise and line 2 anticlockwise), stopping at every important building, giving you the opportunity to take a closer look at some places.

Even though the Ringstraße is so famous, you will not actually find a road of this name on your map, because every part of the **Ring** has its own particular name referring to its purpose (e.g. Opernring, Burgring). I'd suggest to start the tour on Stubenring at the Underground stop U3 Stubentor.

STUBENRING / Dr.KARL LUEGER PLATZ

A model of the old city encircled by its city walls.

Here, right behind the monument of Dr. Karl Lueger (mayor of Vienna under Emperor Franz Joseph I) we can see remains of the **city walls,** which were excavated when the Underground station was built in 1985. In front of the city walls is a model of the city of Vienna encircled by its walls and with St. Stephan's in the centre. The **Stubentor (Chamber Gate)** was the oldest part of the city walls, built between 1195 and 1250 and was renovated and re-enforced after the first Turkish siege in 1526, saving the city from being overrun in the second siege in 1683. Outside the city gate the large area of water meadows and woods stretching as far as to the Wienfluß river, was called the "Wasser Glacis". This part was later turned into Vienna's first public park; the Stadtpark.

STADTPARK

The **Stadtpark (City Park)** covers an area of approx. 65 000 m² along the outer side of the **Parkring.** It offers both young and old a chance to relax in its well maintained historic gardens laid out in an English country style more than a hundred years ago. A children's playground of about 34 000 m² was added more recently on the other side of the Wienfluß; the little stream that separates the two parts of the Stadtpark which used to be a dangerous river before being regulated. Nowadays most of the stream runs underground through the city.

Donau Nixe (Danube Mermaid)

The little statue of the **Danube Mermaid,** which stands in a small square hidden among some rose bushes near the bridge over the stream, reminds us of its times as a free flowing river in which not only fish lived, but also the dangerous "Waterman and his daughters", the nymphs and mermaids.

THE WATER-MAN

People who lived in the little villages along this dangerous river used to warn their children about the wicked Water-man who lived there. It was said that the Water-man sat on the river-bank combing his wet, green hair with a golden comb trying to lure little boys and girls close to the water's edge. Once there he could easily pull them down into his cold water-palace, decorated with ceramic pots containing the souls of his previous poor victims.

117

Once a boy wanted to impress his friends by showing them that he could trick out the Water-man and cross the river, even though he could not swim. He put several air filled ox-bladders round his waist and walked into the water saying that those would keep him afloat. However, when he was in the middle of the river, the Water-man came up from his palace and showed him that he can't be tricked so easily, punctured the ox-bladders and drowned the poor boy immediately.

Another tale is told of a little girl who was picking flowers in the meadow near the river. The Water-man called her to come closer to him at the river bank, where the most beautiful flowers were growing. The girl was saved from his wicked lure because a man, working nearby in the fields, had overheard the conversation and shouted to her: "Run away little girl, the Water-man wants to take you, don't go near him!", and luckily the sun had also weakened the Water-man so that he didn't have the strength left to pull her into the river.

THE DANUBE MERMAID

A mermaid with beautiful golden hair was also said to live in the Water-man's palace. The older fishermen told their sons to watch out particularly for her, because she would rise, choose one of them and lure him into the water by singing him the most tempting songs. Although the young men didn't really believe these stories, many of them vanished in the wild waters of the Danube.

When during the winter months the Danube's waters were covered with a thick layer of ice so that the fishermen could not go fishing, they stayed in their houses near the river to mend their nets and boats for the coming season. One day a fisherman was just telling his son about a beautiful mermaid he had once seen in the distance, when suddenly the door was opened by a mermaid. They both stared at her in fear and shock, thinking that she had come to get them. The mermaid however, told them not to be afraid, since she had only come to warn them that the weather would be changing suddenly, melting the ice and flooding all the villages along the river. They should warn their neighbours and flee inland as far as they could.

A few days later the land alongside the river was in fact completely flooded, but the fishermen's lives had been saved since they had followed the mermaid's warning. They returned after the waters had retreated and rebuilt their villages, feeling happily convinced that the mermaid was in fact their good fairy who would protect them. The young man, who had seen her, however was very sad and longed to meet her again. He sailed on the river for hours, staring into the water and searching for her. This made his father very sad, because he felt that he was losing his son to the mermaid's spell. When fishermen later found his son's empty boat on the river, he knew that his son had found the mermaid and she had taken him to her water-palace forever.

Once the spell of mermaids and water ghosts has left you, we continue our way to a statue in the Stadtpark of a more famous person. Leave the square in the direction of the Kursalon and you soon come to the statue of the celebrated composer **Johann Strauss II,** who had followed in his father's footsteps (Johann Strauss I) by writing more of the already popular waltzes, polkas and operettas. Johann Strauss II, who lived from 1825 to 1899, was not only a composer, but also a successful conductor, often working with several orchestras on the same day. He is said to have rushed from one event to the other and sometimes conducting as many as 6 orchestras in one evening. His compositions are still loved and played at balls and concerts all over the world.

His most famous one: "An der schönen blauen Donau" ("Blue Danube") is the centre piece of the annual New Year's Concert which is seen via television all over the world.

Johann Strauss II at the Stadtpark

In reality the title refers not only to the colour of the Danube (which isn't always blue), but also to that Viennese characteristic of being often sad and blue. Even more romantic feelings are expressed by his waltzes such as: "Gschichten aus dem Wiener Wald" (Tales from the Vienna Woods), or his operetta "Der Zigeuner Baron" (The Gypsy Baron, set in Hungary's aristocratic history). His father composed even more stirring pieces, such as the one called "Radetzky Marsch" (a glorification of Field-Marshal Radetzky and Austria's military past) which is usually accompanied by the audience clapping in rhythm to the music from the first to the last note.

Once you have seen this great Austrian, we walk to the tram (line 1) just opposite the park in front of the Mariott Hotel and continue the tour.

SCHWARZENBERG PLATZ

At the next tram stop, **Schubertring,** you see to the left the fountain **Hochstrahlbrunnen** at the far end of the square, which was built for the opening ceremony of the Vienna water supply lines. Behind this, the memorial of the **Unknown Russian Soldier** towers high above the fountain as a memorial to the many Russian soldiers who died during the Second World War. When Austria was liberated in 1955 after 10 years of occupation, it promised that it would continue to always honour and maintain this memorial.

STATE OPERA

At the next tram stop, **Kärntner Ring,** we arrive at **Kärntner Straße,** which runs from the city centre in the direction towards the southern province of Austria called Kärnten (Carinthia).

 Look to the right as soon as the tram has started again and you see the **State Opera House** of Vienna, where many famous opera singers have performed since its opening in 1868. Its most famous event however, is the annual Opera Ball to which people come from all over the world. The State Opera House was built by the two architects August Siccardsburg and Eduard van der Null and their use of the early French Renaissance style for the architecture of the building, was met with much criticism by the Viennese at the time. When even the Emperor expressed his disapproval, the architect Eduard van der Null was so upset about it that he

committed suicide, greatly shocking the Emperor Franz Joseph I. As a result he never again publicly criticised any of his subjects' works and took on the habit of always commenting: "Es war sehr schön, es hat mich sehr gefreut!" ("It was very nice. I'm very pleased!"), to whatever he was shown.

A little further along the **Opernring** on the right hand side, we see a statue dedicated to the most famous German poet **Johann Wolfgang von Goethe** at the corner with the historic garden of the Hofburg, the **Burggarten (Imperial Palace Gardens).**

BURGGARTEN

If we get off at the tram stop **Burggarten,** we can spend a few minutes there to see the memorial statue of the composer Mozart just inside the main gate. Of course, everybody has heard of **Wolfgang Amadeus Mozart,** the child prodigy who could play the piano perfectly at the age of six, and even started to compose and play the violin before having any lessons.
He was born in Salzburg in 1756 as the second child of the court conductor Leopold Mozart. "Wolferl", being admired for his talent and taken from court to court as the child prodigy by his father, eventually found it unbearable to live as a servant of the Archbishop of Salzburg.

Wolfgang Amadeus Mozart

After many years of unwilling service, and disputes with his employer, he was dismissed by the archbishop and then free to start his own career in Vienna. Although he was overjoyed by the fact that he had finally gained his personal freedom, he found it very difficult to earn enough money to support his wife Constanze and their children. It is sad to say that this great musical talent had to die as a lonely and destitute man in Vienna in 1791. His famous works, like the operas: "Magic Flute", "The Marriage of Figaro", "Don Giovanni" or "Cosi fan Tutte" are still among the most admired and best loved performances at the State Opera.

Taking a little detour to the right we come to a statue of the **Emperor Franz Joseph I,** as if he were walking through the park in the days when the Burggarten was only used by members of the royal family. At the far end of the Burggarten, a range of beautiful tropical palms and flowers are on show in the Palm House. The

Heldenplatz (Heroes' Square)

127

glass and steel construction of this historic greenhouse has been fully renovated recently and it now boasts a modern coffee house as well.

BURGRING - HELDENPLATZ

We continue on foot on the part of the **Ringstraße** called the Burgring, which separates the **Hofburg** buildings on the right from the **Museums** on the left. The complex of buildings immediately to the right is called the Neue Hofburg and was started under Emperor Franz Joseph I, but was too grand a project ever to be finished in its entirety due to lack of funds. The original plan was to connect the buildings of the **Neue Hofburg** on the right hand side with similarly designed buildings on the left hand side of the Ring and to close off the complex with a building towards the **Alte Hofburg,** creating a large courtyard in the middle. The grand buildings on the left of the **Burgring** are now used as the **Kunsthistorisches Museum (Museum of Art History)** and the **Naturhistorisches Museum (Natural History Museum).** The square between these two museums is dedicated to **Empress Maria Theresia,** who we can see seated on a huge throne surrounded by her advisors.

A little further on we see on our right the **Äusseres Burgtor (Outer Gate of the Palace),** which was built

128

entirely by soldiers and is now a memorial dedicated to the unknown war heroes; as is the square behind it which is called **Heldenplatz (Heroes' Square).** The focal point of Heldenplatz are the two statues of famous Austrian heroes on horseback: **Prince Eugene of Savoy** who defeated the Turks and **Archduke Karl** who won the battle at Aspern against Napoleon.

PARLIAMENT

At the other end of Heldenplatz we arrive at **Volksgarten (People's Park)** lying behind a high iron fence.
Looking through the fence on the far side of the Park, in fact on **Dr. Karl Renner Ring** (1st President of the Republic of Austria 1945-1950), we can see the **PARLIAMENT** building, which is designed in Greek classical style.

The **Volksgarten** is especially worth mentioning for its extensive range of many different sorts of rose bushes set in the rectangular square near the main entrance. Hidden behind some rows of trees we can find a white marble memorial to **Empress Elisabeth.**

129

RATHAUS

On leaving the park at the main exit towards the **Burgtheater (National Theatre)** you can walk to our next stop the **Rathaus (Town Hall)** on the **Dr. Karl Lueger Ring.** A short stroll around the **Rathausplatz (Town Hall Square)** will enable us to see statues of the following Babenberger Kings which we have heard of in former chapters: Herzog Heinrich "Jasomirgott" (Duke Heinrich "Jasomirgott"), Herzog Leopold d. "Glorreiche" (Duke Leopold the "Glory") and Herzog Rudolph d. "Stifter" (Duke Rudolph "the Founder").

At the request of Emperor Franz Joseph, the architect designed the new Rathaus building to be lower than the nearby Votive church. However, the members of the town council found a way to ensure that their town hall would be higher than the emperor's church by putting a figure of a town councillor on top of its highest tower. The **Rathausmann** (town councillor) is three and half meters tall, you can see a copy of him in a niche on the square.

The **Rathausplatz** itself serves as a venue for many different events during the year. You may find the square occupied by a circus; or a huge stage for a pop concert; or in winter an ice rink is made where people can skate until late at night. During the months of July and August you can watch operas shown on a huge open air screen. The most important event however for children is the annual advent market, the **Christkindl Markt** in December, where Christmas trinkets, toys, presents and food are sold in a romantic atmosphere.

The new Town Hall "Rathaus"

Taking tram line 1 again will take you past the remains of the city walls called Mölker Bastei on the right and then on the left hand side the University of Vienna.

At the stop **Schottentor (Scots' Doorway),** which used to be an entrance in the city wall near the Scots' Church, look to the left to see **Votivkirche (Votive Church or the Divine Saviour),** which was built in gratitude for the Emperor's lucky survival of an assassination attempt in 1853.

THE EMPEROR'S GRATITUDE

In the early years of his reign, Emperor Franz Joseph regularly walked in the Inner City. On February 18, 1853 while accompanied by one of his adjutants he was attacked with a knife from behind by a young man. His first blow hit the Emperor's neck, but didn't go very deep into the flesh and so the attacker attempted a second blow, but was overwhelmed by the adjutant and held on the ground until the police arrived. The attacker, who was identified as a young Hungarian tailor who hated the Emperor's rule over his homeland, was sentenced to death and executed.

It took the Emperor several weeks to recover from his injury but as soon as he was able to leave the house again he went to St. Stephan's Cathedral to thank God for his survival and promised to build a church in gratitude.

It took 25 years to build the Neo-Gothic church dedicated to the Divine Saviour, which was finally opened on April 24th 1879, on the 25th wedding anniversary of the royal couple Emperor Franz Joseph and Empress Elisabeth. The grand opening ceremony was celebrated by the Archbishop of Vienna, together with 49 Bishops from the provinces and was also the most glorious event to take place on the recently finished Ringstraße when thousands of people watched the parade.

Our tour of the Ring is almost completed when we pass the building of the **Börse (Stock Exchange),** on the right hand side of the **Schottenring.** As the tram turns from the Schottenring into the **Kaiser Franz Joseph's-Kai** (which completes the Ring along the Danube Canal) we pass the first high-rise-building built in Vienna after the Second World War, the **Ringturm.**

If you look to the right just after the tram leaves the U4, U2 Schottenring stop you will see the eldest church of Vienna, the **Ruprechtskirche,** which is described in chapter 2: "Legends on Foot".

Further along the Danube Canal at the corner of **Kaiser Franz Joseph's-Kai** and **Stubenring** we pass the **Urania,** the original observatory of Vienna, where you can still today go on a guided tour and learn about the stars you see in the sky in a clear night.

The grand building on the left just after the tram turns into Stubenring was originally the **Ministry of War** when it was built just before the outbreak of the First World War in 1918. In front of it is a statue of Field Marshal Radetzky on horseback who was the commander of the Austrian troops in Northern Italy, when this part of Italy still belonged to the Austrian monarchy.

For those interested in Art Nouveau, a visit to the **Otto Wagner post office building,** which we can see set back on the right, is recommended. Those interested in art and architecture of the Biedermeier and Baroque period will find a visit to the **Museum f. Angewandte Kunst (Museum of Applied Art)** worth while and the **Prachner Bookshop** hidden behind the original window facade of the Museum provides all the books on art and architecture that a specialist will expect to find.

At this point we have finished circling the Inner City on the Ring and can get off the tram at the stop U3 Stubenring, just opposite the **Museum für Angewandte Kunst (MAK)** and the Stadtpark.

If you stay on the tram all around the Ring, the tour shouldn't take you much longer than 30 minutes depending on the traffic situation. However, if you choose to stroll through the different parks it may take as much as the good part of an afternoon, to enjoy the sights mentioned here.

DAY TRIPS: PRATER; VIENNA WOODS

PRATER

STARTING POINT
U1Praterstern
Bus 80A, Trams 1, N, O

An afternoon spent enjoying the many different attractions of the **Prater** provides an opportunity for all ages, but especially children, to enjoy Vienna's traditional, leisure and amusement park.

The origin of the Park's name came about because in 1194 the Babenberger Duke Friedrich I gave these river woodlands as a gift to an Italian royal family called de Prato, who changed their name to Prater. In 1546 Emperor Maximilian II, who was a very keen hunter and not wanting to be disturbed, had the area fenced in and guards posted to keep common people out.

However, in 1766 the "people's Emperor" Joseph II, donated these Royal Hunting Grounds to the people of Vienna and a day out in the Prater immediately became very popular.

The amusement park **Wurstel Prater** or **Volks Prater** (People's Prater) at the beginning of the Prater got these two different names from the people of Vienna, because its main attraction used to be a puppet show for small children in which the **"Wurstel"** (Punch

136

Vienna's giant wheel: Riesenrad

and Judy) were the main characters. This puppet theatre was put up next to the restaurants so as to keep the children amused while the parents enjoyed eating, drinking and dancing.

Nowadays the Wurstelprater is not only popular for the **Riesenrad (Giant Wheel),** built by the English engineer Walter Basset for the World Exhibition in 1896; but also for the many roundabouts, swings, helter-skelter, race tracks, pony rides, amusement halls, ghost trains and rocket rides which will test the strength of your stomach after a heavy meal at one of the many restaurants.

China Man guarding the old roundabout.

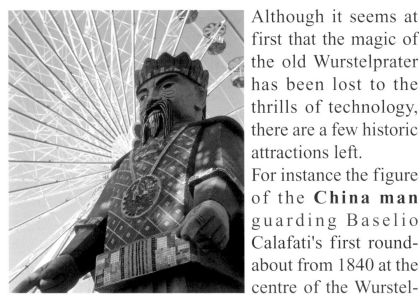

Although it seems at first that the magic of the old Wurstelprater has been lost to the thrills of technology, there are a few historic attractions left.

For instance the figure of the **China man** guarding Baselio Calafati's first round-about from 1840 at the centre of the Wurstelprater; the Hochschaubahn (big-dipper); the miniature train called the **Liliput - Bahn** that takes you with its huffing and puffing steam locomotive on a round trip of the main Prater as far as the football stadium.

Small girls enjoying the old roundabout.

The Wurstelprater however, is just a small part of the huge recreation area called **Prater** which covers an area of approx. 3200 acres between the Danube and the Danube canal.

Its main avenue the **Hauptallee** is app. 4 km long from the Praterstern (U1 stop) to the Lusthaus, a coffee house built 400 years ago. In the meadows and woods of the main Prater you can do everything from relaxing in the sun, flying kites, playing football, cycling and horse riding. A walk along the Hauptallee under the chestnut trees, which were planted in 1537, has always inspired lovers and composers alike when they are in full bloom in spring.

There are facilities for a number of sports such as: a public swimming-pool, which is open from May 1st to the end of September; tennis courts, bowling halls, and even a golf course at the **Freudenau,** which is however more famous for being Vienna's race course called the **Rennbahn.**

Liliput-Bahn

THE VIENNA WOODS

KAHLENBERG - LEOPOLDSBERG

STARTING POINT
**U4 Heiligenstadt
Bus 38a to Kahlenberg
By Car: Höhenstraße to Kahlenberg**

The green hills that encircle Vienna like a half moon from west to east are called the **Wienerwald (Vienna Woods).** A good large scale map of Vienna will enable you to find your way to places for hiking or even mountain biking such as the Lainzer Tiergarten (near Schönbrunn), Schottenwald, Hohe Wand, Dornbacher Forst, Neuwaldegg, the Cobenzel, Sievering, Grinzing and Kahlenberg. There are meadows where you can rest and picnic and playgrounds for the kids.

A typical "Heuriger"

 For those who enjoy a glass of good local wine, a visit to one of the many "Heurigen" inns is recommended, to enjoy a glass of this year's vintage.

141

Kahlenberg and Leopoldsberg

The **Kahlenberg** and the **Leopoldsberg** are the most famous hills of the Wienerwald forming the crescent's sharp end to the north-east. These slope steeply down to the Danube, before the river flows on in wide curves past Vienna and can be seen from as far away as the tower of Saint Stephan's Cathedral, the Riesenrad (Giant Wheel at the Prater), or a bridge across the Danube canal.

Kahlenberg and Leopoldsberg are historically and geographically so closely linked to each other that even their names were swapped in the course of time and Leopoldsberg was named after the castle of the Babenberger Duke Leopold, while its original name Kahlenberg was given to its twin mountain on the left. However, because of their high vantage point they not only provided the Babenberger Dukes with a valuable defensive barrier, they also played a major offensive role in the battle for the liberation of Vienna from the Turks in 1683.

Church on Kahlenberg and Jan Sobieski

A plaque on the front wall of the church commemorates the holy mass celebrated here for King Sobiesky's relief troops before they charged down the hills to attack the Turks on an early September morning in 1683.

We now have a choice of continuing our journey by bus or car over to the Leopoldsberg, or enjoying a short walk of about 30 minutes through the woods along a well paved path via the Josefinenhütte to the top of the Leopoldsberg. Even before you reach the top, you can already see the city spreading out beneath you, lying between the green hills of the Vienna Woods and the Danube. It is well worth going up to the very top to enjoy the view from the place on the castle walls where a stone model of Vienna shows you the city as it looked like when still surrounded by city walls.
By strolling through to the other side of the castle court yard (now a restaurant garden), one gets an excellent view of Klosterneuburg with its impressive Babenberger monastery.

KLOSTERNEUBURG

STARTING POINT
By Train: U4 Heiligenstadt and Schnellbahn
By Car: Via Heiligenstädterstraße

The Monastery of Klosterneuburg was founded by the Babenberger Leopold III "the Saint". The original Romanesque church took 22 years to be built and was consecrated in 1136, just a few days before his death. A legend tells us why he pledged to build this monastery in Klosterneuburg.

"St. Leopold" celebration on November 15th in Klosterneuburg by Zafaurek, Photo Kitlitschka

THE VEIL ON THE ELDER BUSH

Newly married Leopold III and his wife Agnes stood on the castle's balcony admiring the beautiful countryside around them, when a sudden strong gust of wind blew the wedding veil away down into the woods below. Agnes was very sad about the loss of her wedding veil and so Leopold, together with his servants, searched for it for weeks, but they just couldn't find the veil. In desperation, he made a vow that if only he could find the veil, then he would in return build a monastery on that very place.

Some years later when Leopold was out hunting in the woods, he followed his dogs, who led him to a thickly overgrown elder bush. Coming closer, he saw his wife's wedding veil hanging on the bush and gleaming in a heavenly light. To his surprise, the veil was completely undamaged and just as beautiful as it had been years before. Seeing this as a sign of the Virgin Mary, Leopold built the monastery as he had promised and dedicated it to her.

It was named Klosterneuburg (Kloster - monastery, neu - new, burg - castle) as the place was so close to his old castle.

In the 17th and 18th century the original Romanesque church was enhanced with a so called New Building in

Baroque style. One of its two copper domes is decorated with the German Imperial Crown and the other with the Bonnet of the Lower Austrian Canon. Most of the members of the royal court and the monastery fled when the Turks advanced and the monastery suffered great damage during the siege in 1683. However it was fortified enough to provide shelter for the two monks and the village people who stayed behind there.

On a guided tour through the monastery and its precious Baroque royal residence buildings, which include the especially worth mentioning imperial appartments of Emperor Karl VI, we are not only shown and have explained the fortifications and living conditions of the monks and the villagers, but also learn more about the Babenberger dynasty and their rule over Austria. An oil painting in the monastery's museum depicts the scene when Duke Leopold kneeled down in front of the elder bush with the veil on it and experienced the vision of the Virgin Mary above it. The most valuable treasure of the monastery is the **"Verduner Altar",** which is a masterpiece of goldsmith work by Nikolaus of Verdun from 1181, and shows scenes from the Old and the New Testament in 51 enamelled gold panels. The shrine on top of the Verduner Altar contains the remains of Leopold III "the Saint", who was canonised by the Pope in 1485.

Saint Leopold is celebrated every year on November 15th as the founder of Klosterneuburg and the patron saint of Lower Austria. On that day the monastery opens its huge wine-vaults for the public to take part in the barrel sliding festival, where you slide down from the top of the huge **"Thousand bucket barrel"** (approx. 56.000 litres or 1000 buckets) like the landlord did in 1704 in the following legend:

THE LANDLORD AND THE BIG BARREL

Sometimes after the work had been done in the wine cellar, the landlord of the monastery's inn and his workmen would sit together to enjoy a glass of wine and have fun. There was the cellar master who looked after the wine, the cooper who built and repaired the barrels, as well as their apprentice boys and helpers. The cooper in particular was known for his games and the tricks that he played on others. He suddenly said to the newly wed landlord: "You are obviously a real man and the boss of your house, but let me tell you, things will soon change and you too will soon have to do what your young wife tells you, just as all other husbands do. For instance, if your beloved Lehne wanted you to slide down from the big barrel, then you would have to do it whether you wanted to or not!"

The landlord smiled at the idea in disbelief and said: "If I should ever become such an idiot, I would make it a right that in our cellar, every guest should mock me by also sliding down our big barrel."

"Agreed, agreed!", shouted the master cooper and everybody laughed.

The landlord's young wife got to know the story through the help of the cooper and was very upset about it because she considered that her husband's true devotion to her must be very low, since he would not even do such a simple request if asked. She therefore did not want to see her husband anymore, pouted and cried. He could not understand why she was in such a terrible mood so shortly after their wedding and tried everything to make her happy again, but she couldn't accept being together with him anymore. Finally he asked her for the reason of her sudden change in mood and she answered: "What, you don't even know? It was you who said that you don't love me enough to slide down the big barrel if I wanted it!" "But dear wife, why should you want me to do that?", he asked. "Well, I now want you to do it, because you have deeply disappointed me, and if you still love me you must grant me this request as a sign of your devotion." The poor man tried all sorts of ways to change his wife's mind, but he finally had to give in and he agreed to go to the cellar that day late at night, not knowing that his wife had informed his colleagues to witness this test of his devotion. When he still hesitated to make this gesture of reconciliation, she started to cry again and he finally had to admit the whole story: " Lehne please understand that if someone sees me sliding down the barrel, I will become the laughing-stock of the city and everybody will be allowed to slide down as well and laugh at me." He thought that his confession would help him, but Lehne thought otherwise and insisted that it was time he proved his love for her. In the end the landlord saw no other way of escaping the situation and climbed the ladder up to the top of the barrel and came sliding down the other side where Lehne was standing holding a lamp to see him coming down. As soon as he came down, the cellar was suddenly filled with the loud laughter of all his colleagues who were hiding behind the other barrels waiting to see his defeat. The cooper tried to comfort him: "You see, I told you, when a woman wants something the man has to do it. That has always been the case and always will be."

Since that time every guest at the monastery has the right to slide down the big barrel in Klosterneuburg on November 15th. As long as the landlord lived he unfortunately had to endure the mockery of the people, but when he died the right to slide over the barrel was kept on for the enjoyment of everybody who comes to visit the famous old cellars of Klosterneuburg.

In case my stories about the Babenberger knights and their rule over Austria have whet your appetite and you'd like to see more of Austria's historic sights I'd suggest taking a boat trip on the Danube to the Wachau valley, where you are not only spoiled with the view of Austria's most splendid landscape, but you can also visit its famous monasteries at Melk and Göttweig, as well as the castles at Aggstein and Dürnstein.

View of Maria am Gestade and the Kahlenberg

BIBLIOGRAPHY

Richard Rickett, A Brief Survey of Austrian History,
Verlag Georg Prachner, Wien
Richard Rickett. Music and Musicians in Vienna,
Verlag Georg Prachner, Wien
Recheis, Die schönsten Sagen aus Österreich,
Verlag Carl Überreuter, Wien
Nack, Die schönsten Sagen aus Wien,
Verlag Carl Überreuter, Wien
Prof. Leander Petzoldt, University Innsbruck Institute
of Ethnology, Sagen aus Wien
Domkirche St. Stephan, Kirchenmeisteramt, Wien
Veröffentlichte Sagen aus dem Archiv
Chorherrnstift Klosterneuburg, Stiftsmuseum

"Karlskirche" built under Emperor Karl VI

FEEL PECKISH ?
GET A BITE
AT

WIDE SELECTION OF GOODS
EVERYTHING
AVAILABLE FROM

APPLE TO WINE

800
OUTLETS ALL OVER
AUSTRIA
ABOUT 250 IN
VIENNA

Open Mon. - Thurs. from 8 am to 7 pm
Friday from 8 am to 7.30 pm
Saturday 7.30 am to 5 pm
ON AIRPORT SCHWECHAT
EVERY DAY; EVEN SUNDAYS
from 7.30 am to 10 pm
FRANZ JOSEFS BAHNHOF
PRATERSTERN BAHNHOF NORD
EVERY DAY; EVEN SUNDAYS
from 7.30 am to 10 pm

The Waltz-king Joahnn Strauss

The British Bookshop

YOUR SPECIALIST FOR ENGLISH
BOOKS - VIDEO - AUDIO

FICTION - NON-FICTION
CHILDREN'S CORNER
LANGUAGE CENTRE

A-1010 Vienna, Weihburggasse 24
Fon : (+43-1) 512 19 45
Fax : (+43-1) 512 10 26
E-mail: britbook@netway.at
www.britishbookshop.at

Open: Monday - Friday 9.30 am to 6.30 pm
Saturday 9.30 am to 5 pm

prachner

BOOKS · MAGAZINES · CD-ROM

BUCHHANDLUNG
FACHVERLAG
BIBLIOTHEKS - SERVICE

ALLGEMEINES SORTIMENT
ARCHITEKTUR U. KUNST

A-1010 Vienna, Kärntnerstr. 30

Fon (+43-1) 512 85 490
Fax (+43-1) 512 01 58
E-mail service@prachner.at
www.prachner.at

prachner   im mak
BOOKS MAGAZINES CD-ROM   ARCHITEKTUR
                                     KUNST
                                    DESIGN
                                   LITERATUR

A-1010 Vienna, Stubenring 5
Fon (+43-1) 512 85 49-50
Fax (+43-1) 710 47 59

Open: Tu., Wed., Fr., Sat., Sun., from 10 am to 6 pm
Thursday from 10 am to 9 pm, Monday closed.

View of Vienna in 2000 (by Pablik Pictures)